ISBN 9781838320324

Whilst every care has been taken to ensure the accuracy of the information in this book, the passage of time will always bring changes. The author and publisher cannot accept responsibility for errors that may occur, nor shall we be held liable for any loss, damage or accidents incurred whilst following the guidance in this book.

If you have any problems or questions, please email
support@wandering-bird.com

INTRODUCTION

Motorhoming is a funny hobby. There aren't many activities where you spend a LOT of money buying (or renting) a vehicle, only to receive very little instruction on what to do afterwards. You might get a quick handover from the dealer, but you're very quickly set loose on your own.

When we first started motorhoming, we'd already owned boats for several years. We are fairly practical people, confident in our ability to 'figure it out' and we did, for some of it. **For the rest, we made a mess.** We made all sorts of mistakes. Some harmless, some embarrassing and some… well, we'll get to those later.

If we tried to Google how to fix a problem, we'd either end up on a forum where people vehemently disagreed with each other, or we ended up reading conflicting information from some of the biggest names in the industry. We were totally confused.

I remember how overwhelming getting our first van was and trying to find answers to basic questions we didn't even know to ask. After spending ALL THAT MONEY, I was terrified of doing something wrong, causing damage or generally looking like an idiot.

That's how our website Wandering Bird started - a desire to share our experiences and help other people following in our… treadmarks(?!)

None of what I'm sharing here is rocket science. Believe me, if we can do it, so can you. *(And if you can't, there are plenty of people around whose job it is to help you!)*

But, as with any new hobby, you need somewhere to start. A guide or practical advice which you can work through in a sensible manner. That's what we've aimed to do in Motorhoming Made Simple; giving you the knowledge you need to be able to go off and have epic adventures.

Before we get started, I want to give one essential piece of advice: **Be Kind.**

Both to yourself and anyone else you travel with. You're not SUPPOSED to know everything in this book straight away. You WILL make mistakes and mess things up. As long as you don't kill anyone, reverse into a building or electrocute yourself, pretty much everything else is fixable and will become a future funny story and learning point.

Promise.

Sure, someone on a campsite might laugh as you drive right over the front of your levelling chocks and have to start all over again. Or if you try to drive away with your electric cable attached or the sunroof open (all of which we've done… several times!)

But I guarantee they've done something silly at some point too.

We all start this hobby as complete beginners, so don't be embarrassed to BE a beginner. Ask for help from campsite wardens or your dealer. Ask questions in Facebook groups or forums (we have a Wandering Bird Facebook group, which you're very welcome to join.)

Don't let beginner mistakes deter you from one of the best decisions you ever made – getting an adventure wagon! Seriously, you have NO IDEA how many awesome experiences you're about to have and I can't wait to see where you end up.

Buying a motorhome changed our entire lives- let's see if we can change yours too.

If you're on Instagram, feel free to tag me, I'd love to see where you go. You can find and follow us at:

@wanderingbird.adventures

Kat x

(Owner of wandering-bird.com)

Table of Contents

In the Dolomites, northern Italy

Our Story

We never meant to buy a motorhome.

Don't get me wrong: my husband and I didn't just fall over, land in a dealership and suddenly own a van but, in all our conversations about 'future life plans', we'd only ever spoken about going adventuring in boats.

We lived on various sail and motorboats for over 15 years and loved it (most of the time!) I'll admit, lugging down all our shopping from a car park in the middle of a winter storm wasn't fun, nor was being awake at 3am because the ropes just WOULD NOT STOP squeaking.

But we loved the peace of waking up on the water, watching the wildlife and the ever-changing sky. Mostly we loved the freedom to be able to explore and travel whilst taking our home with us. Heck, our very first house together was a 22ft sailboat.

Even when we were younger and had very little money, we always tried to find somewhere we could go exploring on the boat (which was so small I couldn't even stand up straight in it!)

As our daughter Jade grew, our boats grew too. We'd always buy a 'project' *(i.e.- total wreck)* and spend our spare time doing it up before selling it and moving on. I don't think we had a New Year's Eve for over 10 years that didn't involve expanding foam, painting or taking a wall down.

One year, we even cut the roof of the boat off (yes, in December. Yes, in the UK. Yes, it was freaking cold for the next few weeks!)

Then, one October, completely out of the blue, life threw us a curveball. My mother-in-law got sick. Really sick. One day we were all happily chatting about plans for next summer, the next she was in the hospital, then in a coma and then she was gone. It was sudden, brutal and horrible.

My husband was heartbroken (still is), though he did his best to hide it (still does). In an attempt to distract him for a little while, I took him to a local motorbike dealer where he promptly fell in love with a tourer / adventure bike (a Triumph Scrambler, for anyone who knows bikes).

And then I fell in love with one too.

The trouble with watching people you love pass away is that you realise just how SHORT and precious life is. So we bought the bikes and started planning all these adventures we'd been talking about doing for years.

We discovered we could travel further and faster by bike than we could with a boat and a week's holiday wasn't dependent on weather or tide times.

On our first trip abroad with the bikes, we fell in love with riding in Europe; so much easier than the crowded south coast of England where we lived.

The only downside was trying to find somewhere to stay. Hotels were too expensive (our daughter was now too old to share a room with her Dad), but most BnB's are… unwelcoming to bikers.

One day, we literally rode past the answer: a motorhome pulling a trailer with 2 motorbikes on the back. It was the perfect solution; we could travel quickly to wherever we wanted without worrying about taking our daughter on a motorway on the bike, and when we arrive at location, we would have a base with a proper toilet, a hot shower, and a bed with a mattress.

Our first motorhome (a McLouis Tandy) in Switzerland

We bought our very first motorhome three weeks later with little to no planning, research, or knowing what the heck we were doing.

We figured we'd lived on boats for so long that we could work it all out; in some ways we were right, but in many ways, we were very VERY wrong. Our first van was totally wrong for us in almost every way *(but we didn't know that then!)*

We set off for Wales the very next day after we got our first motorhome (which I don't recommend - stay close to home for your first overnight trip!)

We forgot and messed up a lot of things; including getting stuck down a narrow road, having to reverse nearly a mile UP a hill (with a bike trailer leading the way!) and generally did many things that I'm going to suggest you DON'T do (more on those throughout this book!)

But... we LOVED it. Our first trip was 4 days in Wales, our second trip was 10 days in Scotland, then we headed off into Europe. It was on that trip that we found ourselves camped at the top of a mountain in the Swiss Alps, staring up in gob-smacked awe at the Milky Way whilst sipping mugs of delicious hot chocolate. That was the moment everything changed.

We agreed life was too short and we weren't doing enough of the things which made us happy.

So, we decided to change it. We came home, started saving like crazy people and realised my husband could do a lot of his work from the road and that we could live and travel on his wage.

I left my job as an Air Traffic Controller (possibly the scariest thing I've ever done!), we kitted out our next van and, less than a year later, we headed off again into Europe.

That first year, we managed to visit 13+ countries and discovered some incredible places, all whilst either home-schooling our daughter or working around her college schedule.

We learned how to balance travel, work, having fun and how to plan a trip so we didn't arrive (or return!) exhausted.

We also bought a dog. A crazy cocker spaniel called Mac who LOVES van life and is never happier than when we stop up a mountain somewhere and he can run wild.

14

Our fur baby, Mac (short for Macallan, because he's the colour of whisky!)

Motorhoming is everything we love about boating- but easier in so many ways. You can visit incredible places, choose to stay in campsites with convenient facilities, or choose to stay at the top of a mountain with no one around except wildlife and the Milky Way *(and possibly a few wolves- we heard the snuffling in the dark!)*

I could spend the next 700 pages waxing lyrical about how fun it is, our favourite adventures and silly things we've done (#alwayslearning), but you've got your own van to figure that all out in.

It doesn't matter whether you're like us and want to escape the rat race as soon as possible, if you've been patiently saving up and waiting for retirement or if you bought a van to enjoy trips with the kids.

It doesn't matter whether you're a cool surfer VW owner (which is what I am in my heart- despite not being able to surf!), or whether you're able to afford one of these top-of-the-line luxury motorhomes, with a Smart car in the garage.

Getting out on the road is getting out on the road, and anyone who feels that pull is part of a unique, full of intrepid explorers.

We're so excited to help you make the most of your adventures and help you get started.

So, grab yourself a coffee (or something stronger!), and let's dive in!

Motorhome / Campervan terminology

Throughout this book, I'll use the term motorhome, camper, campervan, and van (and probably several others!) interchangeably (listing them all each time will get annoying for us both!)

Pretty much everything we talk about in terms of motorhomes can also be applied to campervans, campers, smaller RVs and even parts for caravans (particularly the sections on trip planning and campsites).

A note on COVID

The world is a different place now than it was before 2020. There are new rules and guidelines we need to follow which are changing CONSTANTLY.

It's impossible to predict what might happen in the future, or what the rules might be as you're reading this.

Therefore, we're going to act throughout this book as if there are no COVID restrictions in place (fingers crossed!)

Having said that, nothing we say is meant to encourage you to break any government guidelines or rules. The information we provide here is to help future and safe travel for all, not to promote anything illegal or which might compromise your own or someone else's health.

Thanks for being a responsible traveller.

Choosing the RIGHT vehicle for YOU!

This book is designed to help motorhome or campervan owners make the most of their new vehicle.

If you don't already own your adventure vehicle and you'd like some help with choosing the best vehicle for YOU, you might find our 'Get it Right' buying guide useful (don't worry, this book will still be very helpful once you've got one!)

You'll find our buying guide on the Wandering Bird website, or at this web address:

https://wanderingbird.thrivecart.com/get-it-right-guide/

Getting the most from this guide & QR codes

There is a huge amount of information in this book and many of our recommendations involve some form of tool or a useful bit of kit we love. Of course, over time, those items could change.

This book started life as a digital PDF guide, with plenty of links to helpful resources and additional information. Obviously, in printed form that's much harder, but I've included QR codes throughout when I think you'll find them useful.

To use these, all you need to do is point the camera of your smart phone at the code box, and it will bring up a weblink (usually to a page on the Wandering Bird website.) There, you'll find resources and other info to help you further.

We've made the size of this printed book small, so you can tuck it easily into a pocket or cupboard on the van, ready for whenever you need it. We hope you treat it as a helpful companion, well-thumbed and scribbled in the margins as you find your own way of doing things which works for you.

Right- let's get on with it!

PART 1- COLLECTING YOUR VEHICLE

The day you collect your new motorhome or camper is always exciting. It doesn't matter whether it's a brand spanking new vehicle, or a 'new to you' one; all that time spent planning, researching, and debating is about to become real. The possible adventures and places you could go are never-ending.

The day will be exciting, but it can also be nerve-wracking, especially if you've never owned or driven a motorhome / large vehicle before. You've just spent a lot of money and it's perfectly normal to be nervous.

For this reason, it's important to be as prepared as possible, especially if you're going to collect your van, rather than getting it delivered to your house. Being prepared will make you feel calmer and a bit more 'in control' and you also won't forget something important in all your excitement / mild terror.

Things to do before collection

It doesn't matter whether you're buying from a dealer or private seller, you MUST do the following before you collect your van, ideally before you even arrive at the pick-up location:

- HPI check on the vehicle you're buying
- Make sure you are legally allowed to drive the vehicle

- Insure the vehicle for all required drivers to drive it on the road
- Make sure it has an in-date MOT
- Arrange tax for the vehicle (if necessary)
- Know where you're going to keep it

On top of all the above, don't forget that you will need a way to get your other vehicle back from the collection point- i.e., if you drive there, how will you get your car home as well as the motorhome?

You'll probably need at least two people for logistics, although it can be helpful to have two people in the motorhome too, so asking a relative or friend to drive you there is a good idea.

Alternatively, get a taxi, train or lift to collect your van so you don't need to worry about a second vehicle at all.

HPI check

If you're unfamiliar with the term, an HPI is a Hire Purchase Investigation, and it checks for vehicle history and any outstanding finance against the vehicle (loans with an outstanding balance on them.)

If you buy a vehicle which has not had any loans paid off in full, you run the risk of losing the vehicle if it is reclaimed by the finance company or you could end up in an expensive legal battle. Either way, it's not fun.

DO NOT SKIP THIS CHECK. I don't care if you are buying the van from your parents, brother, best friend or long-lost second cousin- do a check to see if there is any outstanding finance on the vehicle. And do it BEFORE you pay the full amount of money.

If there is an outstanding balance (common on more expensive vehicles if people have used finance to buy them), do a second check to make sure it has been cleared off before you collect.

DON'T trust the seller to do it (even if they are an approved dealer) and don't trust any HPI check paperwork they show you: do your own check!

We use the website hpicheck.com and it costs around £19 for a full check, which is well worth the peace of mind.

Can you legally drive the vehicle?

Admittedly, you should have done this research BEFORE you agreed to buy the vehicle, but better late than never. If you're buying a vehicle with a maximum gross weight of less than 3.5 tonnes, you should be fine with a full driving licence if you're UK based (other countries may differ).

Of course- getting insurance on the thing might be a different matter- I know of people both too old or too inexperienced to get insurance on the motorhome they wanted.

If you are buying a vehicle with a maximum gross weight of OVER 3.5 tonnes, you will need the C1 classification on your licence.

If you took your test before the 31st December 1996, you should have the C1 category automatically on it. Be warned, most people find their ability to drive anything over 3.5t expires at 70 (and it's often very difficult to get it extended), so if you're planning to buy a vehicle for retirement, please take this into account.

If you took your test on or after 01 January 1997, you will NOT automatically have the C1 classification and will need to take a separate test.

TIP: If you do need to do this in order to drive the motorhome you want, look for a driving school which allows you to learn on minibuses, rather than on 7.5t trucks- much easier to pass!

You can find out everything you need to know and check what you are able to drive on the gov.uk website.

Motorhome Insurance

Let's be real. Getting insurance is a pain.

Nobody wants to pay it or wants to input their details 5,0000,000 times into various search engines to get a quote, only to discover that the provider doesn't cover you if you're under 25, or over 60 or because of previous claims.

However… you need insurance.

And you need it BEFORE you collect your vehicle so that you are legally allowed to drive it home or to the place of storage.

Here are some tips to make it a little easier (and hopefully cheaper!) for you.

Do you need separate Insurance? Yes. Just like with a car, you MUST have insurance unless your vehicle is SORNed, which you can do through the DVLA.

And yes, it's a separate policy to your car or motorbike insurance. Some brokers allow you to use any no-claims bonus years you've accumulated on a car or bike, but some don't, so the first year or two of premiums could be quite expensive.

The three common levels of insurance for motorhomes are:

Third party – the bare minimum level of cover you need. This only covers the costs of compensating other people for any injury or damage you cause to them or their vehicle. YOU or your vehicle are not covered in any way.

Third party, fire & theft – this is similar to third party cover, but also includes insurance against your motorhome being stolen or damaged by fire.

Fully comprehensive – this includes everything offered in third party, fire and theft, and also covers accidental damage or destruction to the motorhome. You often have some level of personal protection and contents cover in these policies too.

Many providers also offer foreign usage cover for Europe, ranging from 30 days all the way up to 365 (NOTE: that doesn't mean YOU can be in Europe for 365 days, just that your vehicle can.)

If you're not planning to visit Europe within the next 12 months with your van, look to find a policy which doesn't include this as it could end up being cheaper for you.

Another way to reduce the cost of your policy is to increase the excess you'll have to pay if you make a claim. The amount of this depends on your policy and is usually customisable when you buy.

What type of motorhomes / campers can be insured?

You can cover pretty much anything with the right policy. In the UK, you can insure motorhomes, campervans, converted vans, American RVs, old school buses and pretty much anything in-between.

The only difference is what it costs, and some vehicles or situations may need a specialist broker to find a good quote, which is what we did as we needed something to cover the motorhome for long trips (pre-BREXIT) and the motorbikes both on and off the trailer.

A converted campervan can be tough to insure. Many brokers prefer to say "no" than to carry the risk. Again, a private broker who can talk to the underwriters and arrange a policy for you, rather than an automated website might be a better choice for this.

Another consideration is if you will be living in your vehicle full-time. This will need specialist insurance; there are a few companies in the UK offering this but it's worth shopping around before you commit as prices vary hugely.

Things to consider when insuring your motorhome:

- What level of cover do you want?
- How much is your motorhome / camper worth, and can you afford to replace it?
- Do you want 'new for old' cover? (This is often more expensive).
- Do you need cover in the UK only, Europe for a short time or Europe for a longer time? Make sure you're not paying for European cover if you have no intention of going there!
- Is your vehicle modified? For example, have you changed from a manual to an automatic gearbox? That might affect your premiums.

Where are you going to keep your vehicle? Parking it in a secure storage yard is often much cheaper in terms of insurance than parking it on the road.

Security Requirements. Some of the cheapest policies on the market may require you to have trackers or other motorhome security devices fitted. Some of these require a monthly payment for the tracking service. Make sure you take that into account when choosing your policy and comparing costs.

Contents cover. Some contents might be covered on your home insurance policy. But many are not. Be sure to ask questions from both providers so that you know what's covered inside the motorhome when travelling or when it's not in use (assuming you're not going full-time!)

Towing. This is one of my biggest bugbears. Motorhome towing insurance is a pain. We often tour with two motorbikes on a trailer. We ended up in a situation where our motorbikes weren't covered whilst they were being towed on the trailer.

The bike insurance said the motorhome insurance should cover it… and vice versa! We did eventually get it sorted (in writing!) but that's an easy loophole to fall through, so be sure to read the small print. This is one of the reasons we went to a broker.

How to find the right insurance provider

If you don't already have motorhome insurance, there are loads of potential insurance providers in the UK and Europe alone, so finding the right policy can take some time.

Be sure to do your research and don't just buy the cheapest quote: look to see exactly what is and isn't covered first.

7 easy tips to (hopefully) make your insurance policy cheaper:

- Store your vehicle in secure and approved parking. This can save as much as 10% of policy prices.
- Drive less! Tell your insurer if you are only doing low mileage trips each year; this can save some money, but don't lie as they could check!
- Fit a reversing camera or parking sensor- some insurers reduce policies with these devices fitted.
- Fit additional approved security devices but check with the insurer first to see if they will accept them.

- Don't pay for Europe cover if you're not going to Europe with your motorhome. Some policies will charge less for UK coverage only.
- Build up your no-claims discount. Some insurers offer discounts against previous car no-claims bonus, which is helpful to new motorhome owners.
- If you have a campervan, make sure it's classed as a leisure vehicle and not a commercial one as insurance for leisure vehicles is often cheaper.

Common exclusions in Motorhome Insurance

Here are some things which are often not covered by motorhome insurance, so do check the small print. If in doubt ask them for clarification, especially if you plan to live in your vehicle.

Full-time motorhome living: If your motorhome is your only residence and you live in it full-time, many providers will not insure you. Some people have recommended Comfort Insurance as a good option, but we've never used them personally.

Mould & Mildew: This is often seen as negligence by the motorhome owner, and therefore is not covered by most policies. (We cover tips for stopping this in the maintenance section).

Water damage / burst pipes: If you leave water in your system over winter and a pipe bursts due to the low temperatures and causes damage, many policies don't cover you. Be sure to prepare your vehicle for winter or if you're not going to be using it for an extended period of time (see part 8).

Unforced Entry: If you leave your motorhome unlocked or leave a window ajar and someone breaks in and steals something, you will likely not be covered.

Vermin Infestations: Infestations from rats, mice and other pests are not usually covered, nor is any damage they cause.

Trade Use: If you use your motorhome for business, it becomes a trade vehicle and needs a different type of insurance policy.

Wear and Tear: General wear and tear is not covered by motorhome insurance.

Motorhome & Campervan Breakdown Cover

We always recommend that you have good level of breakdown cover for your van. Some insurance providers offer it in their package, but you can also buy a standalone policy for both the UK and Europe cover.

If it is included with your insurance, make sure it covers your requirements. There have been stories of people with motorhomes over 3.5 tonnes breaking down and then discovering their breakdown cover was only for vehicles less than 3.5 tonnes!!

There are also different levels of cover- whether you want 'home start' (don't bother if your vehicle is kept at a storage yard), roadside assistance or repatriation.

I would suggest as a minimum you want to be taken to a nearby garage and want some form of hotel /

accommodation provided if you need to wait while the vehicle is fixed.

Also, if you plan to travel in Europe, make sure you have a way of getting both you and the vehicle back to the UK- we know several people who have had their motorhomes stuck in Europe and couldn't get them back without a lot of fuss and expense.

MOT & Tax

You need to have an in-date MOT for the vehicle before you drive it unless you are planning to drive it straight to the test centre. We always make getting a new 12-month MOT a condition of purchase.

Also, as soon as you complete the paperwork, the tax of the vehicle becomes your responsibility. Don't forget, even if the vehicle is taxed currently, it doesn't transfer with the sale like an MOT does. YOU still need to arrange to pay your own tax in your name.

Vehicle tax is something we often wait to do until we're collecting. It's very easy to set it up online and I prefer to check the paperwork again first and make absolutely sure the vehicle is correct (and the registration number is right) before we pay the tax.

You can check the MOT and tax status of a vehicle on the gov.uk website and set up monthly / annual payments for tax which give you instant cover.

Where to keep your motorhome

There are many places to store a motorhome / camper, which broadly fall into three main categories:

- At home on the driveway
- On the street
- Private storage

If you're planning to store at home, make sure the vehicle will fit where you need it to, especially if your driveway is tight. Don't forget to include bumpers, bike racks and height in your calculations, as well as 'swinging room' to get in & out of the drive.

If you need a permit for street parking, make sure you remember to get one before collection day so you can park up.

If you're planning to put your van into storage, you will almost definitely need to pre-arrange that. Some places (like near us on the south-coast of England) have waiting lists for the best places- sometimes the wait is over a year!

There are many different types of storage facilities. Some offer CCTV, locked gates and even a tap to fill up with water. Others are little more than a gravel patch on someone's farm. Expect to pay around £60-80 a month for storage but, for us, it is worth the peace of mind. (Also, it might mean you can buy a bigger motorhome than you thought as it doesn't need to fit on a driveway!)

We always prefer to find a storage yard with 24h access which is much more useful if we're planning an early-morning ferry or want to escape for a last-minute weekend away. We also like to make sure they are approved by our motorhome insurance; there is no point paying for something which is going to make the premiums increase even higher.

Most storage facilities have rules about washing your vehicle and many don't even have a tap, so you won't be able to fill up with fresh water before your trip. It's also not possible to plug into electric at most of them, so you'll need to keep visiting all year to check the batteries etc. (more on that later.)

Having said that, the upsides to having your vehicle secure and out of sight is worth the monthly payment and the inconvenience of no water. But it's a personal choice; do what's best for you.

In the Dolomites, Italy- one of our favourite places

Things to buy before collection

I know, I know. You buy a motorhome and suddenly, your wallet is open and you're buying STUFF.

So. Much. Stuff.

You should have seen our spare bedroom before we collected our first van- it was FULL! However, unless you're going straight from the dealer / seller and out onto an adventure (which I don't recommend), you don't need to bring all that stuff with you when you turn up to collect your van.

Literally, all you need (apart from yourself, your phone and your wallet) is a sat-nav and possibly some security devices if you're storing it away from home (more on those later).

Motorhome Sat Nav

A decent motorhome sat-nav is one of the most important pieces of equipment on your van, especially if you will be driving a motorhome instead of a smaller campervan.

Always get one which you can programme with your vehicle's weight and dimensions so it can help you avoid low bridges, narrow lanes and places which just aren't suitable for your van.

In saying that, just remember no device is 100% fool proof and your sat-nav may potentially direct you down an 'unsuitable' road from time to time so keep an eye out for low bridge or narrow road warnings!

Motorhome Security Devices

We highly recommend getting a couple of security devices both for whilst you're out travelling AND for while you're not, especially if you will be keeping your van at home or in a storage yard.

Remember, there are 2 types of thieves: professional and opportunistic. Your aim is to make your vehicle look like 'too much work' so the opportunistic and/or 'lazy' thieves move on to an easier target.

Sadly, professional thieves are a different story. Most of them can overcome nearly any security device terrifyingly quickly. Your goal is to make your van look like too high a risk for the short amount of time they have.

If you park your vehicle on your drive or on a street, consider fitting 2 or 3 very visible devices to deter them as much as possible.

A heavy-duty steering lock can be useful. Same for an outside wheel lock, although sadly both are easily overcome by those who know how. But a deterrent is better than your van looking like an easy target.

CCTV stickers are surprisingly effective, as is having a wireless security camera inside the vehicle. We use an Arlo System, which is battery powered and brilliant.

A tracker is great for your insurance but doesn't do much to deter thieves, especially if they know how to overcome them. So don't rely on that too much.

Extra door and window locks are a great idea - we've installed an additional lock onto our motorhome habitation door.

We are also able to turn our front seats (the driving ones) around, so we lock them in the backwards position using a heavy chain and padlock. Anyone stealing the vehicle would have to drive with the chair backwards until they can cut through the chain.

You can also get a 'clutch claw', which stops the pedals being accessed and are (apparently!) remarkably effective.

If you're keeping the vehicle at home, putting a security bar in the driveway is a great idea- make it as visible and awkward as possible.

Checks to do on collection

Once you arrive at the dealer / private seller, have a good look around the vehicle again first. Make sure there are no new scratches, dents, or other new problems before you sign on the dotted line.

If you asked for work to be done (such as a solar panel or bike rack to be fitted), be sure to check it properly. Try and arrange your collection time for the morning or early afternoon, so you don't feel rushed or pressured by closing time. (Also, this means you should be able to leave before rush hour which is always useful for your first trip!).

You're spending a lot of money, so be 100% sure before you sign any paperwork.

Before you leave, make sure you have the following paperwork signed & ready:

- V5c slip filled in correctly by the seller / dealer

- Warranty info (if any)- you'll probably need to update this with the company yourself when you get home
- Service history for motorhome
- Receipt for purchase- make sure your details and the Registration number are correct
- Instruction Manuals for appliances if there are any (not all owners keep these, but be sure to get whatever paperwork there is)

When you buy a used motorhome from a dealer, you will usually be provided with an essential kit starter pack possibly containing the following (although the exact list will vary based on what you agreed):

- Freshwater hose
- Electric cable
- Maybe levelling ramps / chocks (but not always).
- 2 x Keys for everything- check they all fit! It's easy for dealers to make mistakes and accidentally put the wrong keys with the wrong van.

Remember, you may have automatic locking doors on the cab (with the fob), but the habitation door in most motorhomes needs to be manually locked- don't forget this!!!

Make sure you check everything thoroughly before you depart. Any dealer worth their salt will give you a full handover- particularly if it's your first motorhome.

Ask as many questions as possible during the handover. Make notes about anything which seems pertinent, particularly important things like emptying the toilet / waste, filling water, gas, cooker, fridge, and battery.

You might also like to film the handover if you've never had a motorhome before. Things like removing the toilet cassette or opening the waste taps can be tricky to figure out if you don't know and referring back to a video can be really helpful.

Driving the motorhome for the first time

Ok, here is it- your big moment!! You're about to pull away in your first motorhome.

STOP.

Take your time. This is not the moment to impress people with your amazing boy (or girl) racer skills. If you've never driven a motorhome before, it can feel incredibly intimidating- more so than you might expect.

Here are a few things to do before you even start the engine:

- Set up your seat so it's comfortable
- Check the mirrors are correct for you
- Look at your FUEL status- you'd be amazed how many people run out of fuel on their first motorhome trip!
- Check clutch bite point & brakes (assuming it's a manual and not an automatic!)

36

- Check where the hazard lights are... just in case
- Make sure you know how to reverse- there's a high chance you'll need this on your first trip, even if it's just to park up.

Take your time looking around inside the cab and familiarising yourself with the indicators and switches. You'll probably have a radio and heating, possibly AC, door locking switches, cruise control and a speed limiter. These, of course, will be dependent on the age and model of your van.

The driver and passenger seat may or may not swivel around to face the rear. If they do, check they are locked in the forward-facing position before you start driving- you don't want to go around a corner and start swinging!

You might also see blinds in the windscreen- these pull together or pull up to give privacy in the evenings, but make sure they're securely retracted when driving.

Tips for driving 'the beast'

Driving a motorhome is not like driving a car. For a start, you're a lot higher up. This is great for looking at the views and seeing over hedges and walls, but it does take a little getting used to.

Take the time to adjust your seat and driving position. You should be able to adjust the height of the seat, the steering column, back support and arm-rest height.

Also, a motorhome is likely to be much noisier than you might otherwise expect- especially on that first trip where everything is empty and you haven't had time to stop the rattles (there's a whole section on that in Part 3!).

REMEMBER YOUR WIDE ASS. Most motorhomes and some vans will be wider than a car and your road positioning will naturally need to alter. Take your time to find new 'cues' on the road, such as where you line up with the white line or along the kerb.

You may notice your motorhome wing-mirrors have two different mirrors in them, at slightly different angles. Take your time to set these up so they suit you- they're designed to try to eliminate any blind spots.

Similarly, you might find you have no rear-view mirror at all, especially if you have an end-bathroom (and therefore no rear window). If this is the case, you'll have a rear-view camera where the rear mirror should be; take your time to set it up and make sure it's working correctly so you can see behind you. If your van doesn't have one, I would highly recommend fitting one when you collect (or ask the dealer to fit one for you before collection.)

Also, you need to think about the height of the van. Suddenly, you'll notice height barriers at all your favourite stopping points (especially if they're near the coast) and you'll need to learn the roads which avoid narrow lanes and low bridges, but a good sat-nav should mitigate this somewhat.

You'll also need to watch for low / overhanging branches and trees over the road!

Gear changes may be 'lighter' than you might expect, and the gear-change points might be different to what you are used to in a car. Spend some time getting used to what the optimum gears are at different speeds. It might also be a 6-speed instead of a 5-speed. If you have a new-ish van, you may even have a gear change indicator on the dash.

Some motorhomes have cruise control, which works just like it does in a car. Personally, I hate it, but Mr WB loves it and uses it all the time on long journeys, so have a play and see if it's for you.

Remember that you are driving a heavy vehicle and you need to leave appropriate braking distances- much further than you might be used to. You'll also need to start thinking further ahead and braking more in advance.

If you need to change lanes, do so well in advance. If you are overtaking, remember that you have another 7 or 8 metres behind you before you start to pull back in!

Try to anticipate other road users, especially the impatient ones. You will always get some idiot who cuts you up, dives across for an exit or generally drives like a prat. Just let them go and try not to get too wound up; sadly, it happens fairly frequently.

Driving slower and calmly will help. Focus on your own confidence and DON'T let other drivers on the road intimidate you into driving out of your comfort zone or faster than you want to.

If you have a tight corner, or are turning onto a street, remember your swinging circle will be much larger and you will likely have overhang (the part of the van behind the rear wheels.)

Make sure both directions are clear, because you'll probably go over onto the other side of the road- especially if you have a longer vehicle. In some cases, you may have a blind spot for tight corners or junctions, so there will be a possibility that you need to hang back from the stop-point so you can see traffic.

TOP TIP: Know where you are going when you set off out of the dealership or parking area. It's so easy to get it wrong and you don't want to be trying to turn around 5 minutes into the journey!

Beware of any speed limitations which might be applicable due to your unladen weight. If your unladen weight is over 3.05 tonnes (no, that's not a type- 3.05!), then you can only do a maximum of 50mph on a single carriageway (instead of the usual 60).

Motorway maximum speeds are still 70mph, unless you are towing (then it's 60mph and you can't use the outside lane- these laws are for the UK; check the ones for any other countries.)

Don't ignore any beeping sounds when you start the engine. Many motorhomes beep to show you something is wrong, such as the electric cable still plugged in or the exterior steps down. If you're not sure, stop, check, re-check and go again. Slow and steady is how to get home in one piece.

My husband often says that he finds driving our motorhome relaxing and easier than driving a car… but I guarantee your first time will be anything but relaxing!

(If you'd like to see the video of me driving our motorhome for the first time, **you can find it on the Wandering Bird Youtube channel!)**

HOWEVER- just because it's intimidating, doesn't mean you can't do it. Take your time, allow yourself to be nervous but do it anyway.

I know the family might want to join you when you pick up the vehicle, but I highly recommend giving yourself a little time to figure it all out. You got this.

Our second motorhome- Swift 496 in Switzerland

TOP TIP: If you feel comfortable, I highly recommend visiting a weigh station on your way home, or at least before you put any 'stuff' into your van. That way, you'll know how much payload you have- more explanation on that coming up!

PART 2- GETTING TO KNOW YOUR NEW VEHICLE

Congratulations- you got the beast home in one piece (hopefully!) Now it's time to start delving into all the various systems and understanding the home on wheels you've just purchased.

Obviously, there are hundreds of makes and models of vans on the market, so I can't give you a step-by-step guide to all your systems (that's what your manual is for), but I can give you an overview to help you feel more comfortable with what to do and how to get started.

One of the most useful things you can do, if you are keeping your motorhome on your driveway, is to spend a night or two in it. Yep, right there on your drive. You can test all the systems and check that the lights, fridge, oven, gas, heating and everything else works.

If this is an option, do it- even if you don't usually keep your van at home. Spending time familiarising yourself with your motorhome will make things much easier later on.

However, I know many people are unable to keep their van at home and they'll need to do all their checks when staying on a campsite. If this is the case, don't pick a campsite too far from home. I've included an overview of your motorhome systems here, but a practical guide on what to do when you arrive at a campsite is in Part 5.

Weight and Payload

One of the first things we recommend doing with any new van, before you put ANY more kit on/in it, is to visit a weigh bridge / weigh station. If you're confident enough to do this on your trip home from the dealer, that's the perfect time- get the vehicle weighed with absolutely nothing else inside it apart from you (and your partner if they're joining you on your travels).

It's important to know what your vehicle weighs when empty of 'stuff'. That way, you know exactly how much the difference is between what your MAXIMUM weight allowance is and what your vehicle ACTUALLY weighs when empty.

The alternative option is to stock up your vehicle with everything you want to carry, fill the water and fuel tanks and THEN take it to the weighbridge. The problem with this is it's easy to be overweight and if you drive your vehicle overweight your insurance is not valid. So be very careful doing it this way.

Weighbridges are pretty easy to find and there's usually several in each county in the UK, certainly near big towns as lorries need to use them regularly. All you do is find your nearest one (using the local council website), phone them up and ask to use their weighbridge.

Many of them are run by the local council and there's usually a small charge. Bear in mind that, if you have opted to load up your van before weighing it and you go to a weigh station, there may be an infringement charge involved if you are overweight.

If you're based outside the UK, I'm sure there will be something similar somewhere near you. Your local town hall or office should be able to help.

Understanding Motorhome Weights

This is all well and good, but WHY do you need to know? What does payload even mean?

I'm about to throw a load of acronyms at you. You'll be pleased to know that there are only a couple you really need to worry about, but it's useful to know what the rest mean too:

MIRO- Mass in Running Order: The weight that the manufacturer THINKS your vehicle should weigh when it leaves the factory. This usually includes everything needed to drive the vehicle, such as a tank (or a portion of a tank) of fuel, a driver (average 75kg) and fluids in the engine.

The MIRO is also called the 'unladen weight'; nothing else is in the vehicle- no water, gas, solar panel, pots, pans, bedding or any other gear. And no other passengers or pets.

However, it's a well-known fact that there is often a difference between the manufacturer's MIRO and the actual weight of the motorhome without any gear, not to mention if you happen to be a driver who doesn't weigh exactly 75kg!

Also, many motorhomes ordered from a factory (or bought second-hand) have extras fitted like an awning, solar panel, bike rack or tow bar and it's easy to see how people get so confused by what their motorhome ACTUALLY weighs- and therefore how much you can put in it.

Even if you weigh every single thing you pack, if you don't know the exact starting point, you're going to get into trouble. **So, we recommend ignoring the published MIRO and taking your van to a weighbridge whilst it's empty, so you know where you're at.**

MTPLM- Maximum Technically Permissible Laden Mass (i.e.- the maximum weight your vehicle is allowed to be and still be legal on the road.) You'll usually find this information on a plate somewhere either near the driver or passenger door, or in the engine bay.

Don't forget, if the POTENTIAL MTPLM is over 3.5 tonnes (3500kg), you will need a C1 licence to legally drive it, even if the ACTUAL weight is under 3.5 tonnes whilst you're driving it.

Payload- The difference between the MIRO and the MTPLM is called the payload. Basically, how much stuff you can carry on your vehicle before it goes overweight and becomes illegal to drive.

Don't forget, payload includes EVERYTHING that you put onto the van.

People, kids, pets, tinned food, water, gas, pots, bedding, surfboards, clothes, towels, shoes, cuddly toys: E.V.E.R.Y.T.H.I.N.G.

Don't worry if your brain is imploding right now. Hopefully, this pretty diagram will help:

MAXIMUM ALLOWED
VEHICLE WEIGHT
(MTPLM)

minus

WEIGHT of vehicle
'in running order'
(MIRO)

= **PAYLOAD**

**(AKA- how much 'stuff' you're
allowed to carry- this includes
people and pets)**

The trick now is to pack your vehicle with everything you need, **whilst staying under your maximum allowed weight.** Trust me, it can be a struggle, but you need to be strict when packing. Think "do I really need this?" about every item you add.

Some people choose to up-plate their motorhome, to give them more payload. This is fine, but there are also some downsides to having a vehicle over 3.5tonnes, such as speed restrictions in both the UK and Europe, needing a C1 licence and increased toll costs in some European countries.

It's a weigh-up (ha: pun intended) over which option is best for you. We chose to downsize from our second motorhome (which was over 3.5t) to one under 3.5t as it made life easier for us, especially with only 2 people and a dog.

It also meant I could drive the van without needing to do another test. If you have kids or more pets, you might not have much of a choice about going over 3.5 tonnes and this will affect the vehicle you choose to buy.

Small motorhome & campervan owners- don't assume your vehicle MTPLM is 3.5tonnes. Many smaller vehicles have a lower weight limit, often 3.3t or e less. Check your vehicle plating and paperwork carefully.

NOTE: I've never seen a weight check for motorhomes in the UK, but we HAVE seen several across Europe, especially in France. If you're pulled over and found to be overweight, you will need to leave things on the side of the road until you are under the max limit- and then drive off and leave them there. You could also be fined heavily.

But, most importantly, your insurance will be invalid if you're found to be overweight, so it is a big deal and worth paying proper attention to.

We'll share some tips for packing your motorhome shortly, but first let's get to grip with the physical systems in your vehicle.

Motorhome Systems

Your motorhome is literally a home on wheels and many of the systems you'll find inside are similar to what you might expect in a house.

However, UNLIKE a house, your van isn't connected to any mains services (unless you plug it in to an electric hook-up.) There is no mains electric, no toilet or waste removal, no never-ending water supply; every resource you have and use has to be collected, stored and measured.

Of course, if you are on a campsite or at home and plug your electricity lead into the mains, or connect to a water tap, you'll have access to these. Even then, it's good to be aware of what you're using and how much.

Let's break each system down into more detail:

Power and Electrics

There are three main electrical power sources in your motorhome:

- Mains electric power
- Leisure Battery
- External source (generator, power-bank or solar)

Don't forget, if your motorhome isn't connected to mains using the electric cable (either EHU – electric hook up or a generator), you will NOT be able to use 230v appliances, like microwaves, toasters, hair dryers or electric kettles. The 3-pin plug sockets (if you have a UK van) won't work either.

Even if you are plugged in, most campsites won't be able to handle the power requirements you would need if you turned every 230v device in your van on at the same time; you'll blow a fuse, either just for your own pitch or potentially for the entire site. You don't want to be that van!

So, first important lesson- you need to be careful with how you use electrical power in your van.

The only power you'll be able to use when you're NOT plugged into mains is 12v, such as cigarette / USB sockets. We'll talk most about those shortly.

Mains

As briefly mentioned above, you CAN use mains (230v) appliances in your van- as long as you have the appropriate power source.

The most common way to get this is via your electric cable, by plugging your van into an appropriate socket at a campsite or at home.

Plug in the outside electric cable (usually orange) at the MOTORHOME END FIRST, and then attach it to the power / electric box on the site. Otherwise, you're walking around with a lead holding live electricity.

Similarly, when you want to unplug, detach from the power source FIRST, then detach from the motorhome.

Again, even with the lead connected, don't expect the power on a campsite to be unlimited like in a house. Most campsites have a limit (this is generally 10amps / 16amps), so you need to be thoughtful about what devices you're using at the same time.

(Don't worry- you don't need to do maths. Just don't turn on too much at once. A microwave AND a toaster AND an electric kettle AND a hairdryer all at once is probably too much for most sites.)

IMPORTANT: Don't leave the excess outside electric cable coiled in small coils once it's plugged in- there have been incidents of fire through this. Instead, flake any excess cable into long lengths on the ground (whilst making sure they're not a trip hazard to anyone else.)

It's perfectly ok to leave it coiled up in a locker when not in use- it's only when there's power going through it that you need to be cautious.

230/240v confusion

Whilst we're here, I just wanted to clarify the 230 / 240v situation for anyone who is confused.

The UK has always traditionally used 240v. Europe (or the EU, to be pedantic) wanted to standardise, and they traditionally used 220v. A compromise was reached of 230v.

It's important to understand that nothing actually changed in either the UK or Europe. All your devices still work just the same. There was already a tolerance in the voltages, and the middle ground of 230v is within those tolerances.

So don't worry if your motorhome system says 240v (on an older model) and you have an appliance with 230v (or vice versa)- it will work just fine.

Of course, if you're in or visiting a country with a totally different voltage (such as hiring an RV in the USA), you're going to be unable to use your 230v hair dryer without additional equipment. So be aware of that.

Battery Power

If you have a motorhome or campervan, you've probably got both an engine starter battery (the one which starts your vehicle and is commonly found in the engine bay) and a leisure / domestic battery. Some vans even have two leisure batteries onboard to help increase the power available.

It's normal for motorhome leisure batteries to be sold with the vehicle, so you don't need to worry about buying one (unless it's dead).

NOTE: If you are buying a new CARAVAN, they are often supplied **without** a leisure battery, so you will need to buy one before your first trip.

The motorhome leisure battery is normally NOT found in the engine bay- it's usually somewhere in the camper habitation area. Ours is under the driver seat, but on our last van it was under the floor near the oven. Check your motorhome manual if you're not sure, but this should be something shown to you when you purchase your van.

Let's be honest- most new motorhomers or campervanners don't really think about their batteries until they have a problem. Either the power suddenly dies, or the battery isn't holding a charge, or they arrive at their motorhome or camper after winter to find everything is flat and the battery is dead (we'll talk about how to stop that later on).

A basic level of battery maintenance is important to keep your leisure batteries healthy and happy for their lifespan and make that life span as long as it can be.

Don't worry, you don't need to be an experienced electrician to understand this section. You don't even need to understand amp hours, volts or 'deep-cycle' in order to care for your motorhome batteries.

And no math is required (ok, a teeny tiny bit might be- but I promise you can do it.)

Why do you need a motorhome leisure battery?

The domestic leisure battery provides all the power in the habitation area of your van, whenever you're not plugged in to mains power. It is used for habitation lights, water, toilet, blown-air heating, 12v chargers and anything else electrical.

IMPORTANT (yep, I'm saying it again)– the leisure battery only supplies 12v in your van. So, if you are on battery power, you CANNOT use your 230v (normal 3-pin plug) sockets. So no electrical kettles, or toaster, or microwave (unless you have a motorhome generator or an inverter- we'll talk about that shortly).

In order to be able to provide that power, the battery 'stores' it. Think of it like a bucket of water. You need to put power into the battery. When it's full, no more power can be stored. Then, as you use the power, it's drained down. Once it's gone, it's gone until you replenish the power (using a mains cable, or a solar panel or even a generator.)

The big difference between your camper leisure battery and the bucket of water is that you CANNOT completely empty the leisure battery- doing this will damage it.

You can only use about 50% of the power in your leisure battery before you need to stop draining and start recharging. However, the % readings will depend on the on-board control system you have in your vehicle so be sure you fully understand the system you have.

Can't I just plug direct into mains power all the time?

You could, but the other job of a leisure battery / system is to smooth out irregularities in the power. Without this, you could end up damaging sensitive appliances like TVs due to power spikes or having appliances which need constant power (like alarms or trackers) going on and off regularly due to power fluctuations.

However, if you plan to spend most of your time in your motorhome, campervan or caravan on a campsite, you don't need to buy a top-of-the-range leisure battery as you won't be putting it through as many cycles as someone who mainly stays off-grid.

Why is your leisure battery losing charge?

The other thing to understand is that the power in your battery is not like water in a sealed container. Just like water in a bucket left outside on a warm sunny day, the power in your leisure battery will slowly... disappear *(it doesn't evaporate, but you get my point).*

It's like when you get a static shock and your hair stands on end. Eventually, that energy just... dissipates. The same thing happens to your motorhome batteries (both engine and leisure).

That's why you often return to your motorhome, camper or caravan after winter or a long period of inactivity and find the batteries flat. Even if you've turned everything off and you're convinced nothing is causing the power to drain eventually, over time, the battery will be fully discharged and/or dead.

But don't worry- with proper maintenance and care, you can protect your batteries, even in cold weather, and use them for several years.

Differences between an engine battery and a domestic leisure battery

Engine batteries and leisure batteries are NOT the same and you should buy the appropriate battery for the job.

Engine starter batteries (or car batteries) have thinner plates and are designed for short, sharp bursts of high power in order to crank your engine and get it going.

Leisure batteries are designed for slow release over a prolonged period of time, followed by re-charging. Leisure batteries are sometimes referred to as auxiliary batteries too.

You cannot use a leisure battery in your engine (it doesn't have the 'oomphf' (*technical term!*) to get the engine started), but you could use an engine battery as a leisure if you really REALLY had to.

However, it will not be anywhere near as efficient, and we don't recommend it. There is a type of battery which can do both jobs (an AGM battery), but it's not commonly used for motorhomes (yet!).

How many leisure batteries do you need in your motorhome or campervan?

Great question- and the simple answer is, it depends on your van and how you plan to use it.

On our last motorhome, we had an electric drop-down bed. We loved the idea of this, because it made life easier but, in reality, that thing was stupidly power-hungry and drained our leisure battery so quickly.

For this reason, we decided to fit a second leisure battery into the motorhome (and it's one of the many reasons we eventually decided to simplify and sell that motorhome).

IMPORTANT: You should only put a leisure battery in an appropriate battery compartment. If there isn't space for a second battery, you shouldn't fit one. Also, you will need to declare fitting a second leisure battery to your insurance- they might require you to get it professionally checked.

On our current van and in several vans we've used, there has only been one leisure battery- and it's more than adequate. We love spending time wild camping and we like to stay off-grid away from campsites as often as we can. Even with this, we still don't feel the need for a second leisure battery (although we do have a solar panel, which makes a big difference).

Of course, the more batteries you have, the LONGER you will have battery power for. Note that I say longer, not more. **You can't fit 20 x 12v leisure batteries and suddenly have 240v power to run your microwave**.

How long should a motorhome leisure battery last?

This is a common question, with two possible answers.

Do you mean how long can you use electrical items in your camper before you need to recharge the battery? That depends on the size of your battery and how much power you're using. The more you have switched on, and the more 'power-hungry' the appliance, the quicker the battery will drain.

The number on the battery (for example, '110') refers to 'Amp-hours' (Ah) which is the capacity of the battery- or how much power it can store. In simple terms, it could supply 1A for 110 hours or 10A for 11 hours.

Alternatively, do you mean how long should you keep a leisure battery before buying a new one?

The life of a leisure battery depends on several things:

- How frequently it is discharged
- How deeply it is discharged
- How quickly it is recharged

In order for your battery to last as long as possible, you need to keep it in a good state of charge. If it discharges to a very low level and is left for weeks (or even months, during winter) without being recharged, then it will probably be critically damaged. And then you will need to buy a new one.

With proper care, you can expect a motorhome leisure battery to last around 5 years before it should be replaced.

Of course, if things go wrong or aren't maintained, you could end up buying a new leisure battery every year!

Types of motorhome leisure batteries

There are many types of leisure batteries, and you'll hear all sorts of exciting terms thrown about like lead-acid, wet batteries and lithium ion. Let's have a look at the most popular options.

Lead-acid leisure batteries

The most common form of leisure battery in a motorhome or camper is a lead-acid (although lithium ion is becoming more popular). These are also called 'wet' batteries because… they have liquid inside them.

Lead acid batteries will self-discharge over time. The speed of this depends on make, age etc. You need to be able to keep any eye on electrolyte levels and top up as necessary.

You can get 'open' and 'sealed' lead-acid batteries. Open are the type you have to top up. Sealed are the 'maintenance-free' ones.

Lithium-ion leisure batteries

Lithium batteries are another form of deep cycle battery. They are fully self-contained (maintenance free) and have their own charge manager. Because they don't have lead, they typically weigh around half as much as an equivalent lead acid battery- this can really help with your motorhome payload.

They can also be discharged (fully) and rapidly recharged while retaining a stable voltage level. They are great for motorhome owners who use their vehicles 'off-grid'. They don't self-discharge, are mostly maintenance-free and work well alongside an inverter.

However, they are expensive- as much as five times the cost of an equivalent, good quality, lead-acid battery. So if you don't plan to spend much time in the wilds, you do NOT need one of these- save your money for more important things.

Other types of leisure batteries

AGM batteries – Absorbent Glass Mat batteries have matting between the plates that filter the sulphuric acid inside the battery, making it more resilient and able to withstand a greater number of charging cycles than a typical lead-acid. They can be used as both starter and leisure batteries. The downside is that they are much more expensive to buy.

Gel batteries – These are used in vehicles with a high risk of damage or crashing, such as quad bikes or jet skis. They use gel rather than acid, which reduces the risk if they are damaged in an accident. Some foreign brands of motorhomes or campers are now fitted with these.

Maintenance-free batteries – Conventional batteries have removable caps to allow the acid levels to be checked and topped up with deionised water.

A new option is a maintenance-free battery, which is a sealed unit and cannot be topped up, but doesn't need to be, due to the way it is charged.

Buying & Choosing a motorhome or camper leisure battery

If you find yourself needing to buy a leisure battery for a motorhome, campervan or caravan, it can be a little overwhelming.

As a rough guide, the heavier the battery is, the more lead it contains= increased ability to hold a larger capacity of charge. If you want a deep cycling leisure battery (which you probably do) a heavy battery is a good place to start.

If you are going to be spending most of your overnight stops on motorhome club campsites with mains electric hook-up, an inexpensive battery might be all you need. When connected to a mains supply, the battery is then only there to 'smooth out' the 12V output from the camper's built-in charger.

However, if you plan to use sites without electric hook-up or want to stay off-grid, a good quality, high-capacity battery is essential. Also, if you like to stay in one place for a while (and therefore the alternator isn't recharging the battery), you'll need a good leisure battery for that too.

Only buy batteries that have been manufactured in the last 12 months; older batteries could already have sulphur corrosion.

As well as selecting the best model, you also need to make sure you aren't being sold a starter battery in place of a leisure battery.

The best option to ensure you get a leisure battery suitable for a leisure vehicle is to buy one from the Verified Leisure Battery Scheme.

National Caravan Council Verified Leisure Battery Scheme

This scheme was set up by the National Caravan Council to give owners peace of mind about the quality of their battery. If you buy a leisure battery which displays the scheme's logo, then it has been deemed reliable and fit for purpose by the NCC.

All verified leisure batteries will display the scheme's logo as well as which category it falls into.

NCC Caravan and Motorhome Leisure Battery Verification Scheme

There are three categories of verified leisure battery under the NCC scheme:

Category A – High storage capacity batteries for use by caravan and motorhome users who prefer to operate away from an electrical hook-up point (people who do a lot of off-grid camping).

Category B – Designed for those who use electrical hook-up on the majority of their trips, but also require greater power capacity. Devices such as motor movers (for caravanners) are likely to require a Category B battery even if electrical hook-up is used.

Category C – Verified batteries suitable for use when electrical hook-up is not available for a short time only.

Are all leisure batteries covered by the scheme?

No. At present, only a few manufacturers are included. More are expected to join in the near future, and the NCC will publish updates as and when appropriate.

What affects leisure battery performance?

There are many things which can affect the performance and lifespan of a battery.

Age – Most batteries have a marked decrease in performance after 5 years.

Size – Obviously, the bigger your battery (in Ah, not physical size), the longer you can use your appliances for.

Consumption– Having said that, if you're running a lot of electrical appliances at once, you will drain the battery faster and it will need to be recharged sooner and much more often. The more you do this, the more you degrade performance and life of the battery.

Temperature – Batteries hate cold. The colder the temperature, the worse the battery is going to perform. They really do sulk. If you check your battery, you'll see the 'amp hours' rating will be based on a crazy warm temperature of around 25c, with each degree lower causing a 1% drop in performance.

As an example, a 110Ah battery which is operating in 15c temperature will actually only perform as a 100Ah. *If that's not reason enough to go spend your winters in Spain, I don't know what is!*

The fact of the matter is, you can do calculations all you like, but always err on the side of caution and assume you need to recharge your leisure battery more frequently, and for longer, than you might think.

How to charge a leisure battery on a motorhome or camper

Most motorhomes and campers have several ways of charging the leisure battery:

- Via the mains when on hook-up (battery charger)
- Using the engine (alternator) when on the road- this is often called 'split-charge'
- Solar panel
- Generator
- Wind generators (these are common on boats, but less common on motorhomes or campers)

How to charge a leisure battery from mains / electric hook up

This one is easy. Providing you have a battery charger (more on those below), you just plug in the mains, turn it on (if not already) and relax.

It's that simple, on most modern motorhomes and campervans- the battery will automatically charge from the mains.

How to charge a leisure battery while driving

You charge both your engine and leisure batteries while driving using an alternator. It's highly likely this system is already built into your van and you don't need to do anything special to use it; again, it just happens.

Remember that it takes time to recharge a battery. Running your engine for 15 minutes once a day is unlikely to be enough.

Also, the alternator was never designed to charge leisure batteries- it was designed as part of the engine to recharge starter batteries and that is its main focus.

So you need to allow time for both the starter battery and the leisure battery to be recharged (it's not linear like that, but all you really need to know is it needs time!).

Also, as the battery voltage increases (it gets more charged), the current provided by the alternator will reduce- as it was designed to for the engine battery to stop overcharging. So an alternator is unlikely to fully charge a leisure battery.

Discharge rates

(here's the Maths. DO NOT PANIC...)

As an example, if you have a 100Ah (amp hour) battery (let's ignore the temperature and just assume it's working to 100), and you use (discharge) 50%, you need to replace 50Ah.

Let's say the engine alternator can give 5A to the leisure battery while the engine is running. It will take 10 hours to recharge. That's 10 HOURS of driving. Non-stop.

If you have a bigger battery, or two leisure batteries, you will need even longer.

Luckily, many motorhome battery chargers can provide 15-20amps, so it takes a lot less time: 2 or 3 hours.

Battery Chargers

Using mains electric to charge the leisure battery (and sometimes the engine battery) is common in most motorhomes, but you will need a battery charger. There are several types of chargers available- they do different jobs.

Basic battery chargers

The simplest is a basic unit which gives a fixed output, usually around 13.8 volts. These basic chargers are rarely used in motorhomes these days, because multi-stage chargers are not much more expensive and are much better for the health and lifespan of your battery. Basic chargers are not designed to be left connected long-term.

Multi-stage charger

A multi-stage charger provides charge at different voltages and currents depending on the state of charge of the battery.

These are also called maintenance chargers, although not many are designed to be left connected permanently; you should use a timer or disconnect and reconnect regularly. (Especially important in winter if you leave electric connected permanently).

Usually there are 3 stages of charge:

- Bulk charge mode: gives a maximum voltage and current to recharge the battery quickly. This usually takes it to around 80% full.
- Absorption: Gives a constant voltage but reduces current. Takes it to nearly full charge.
- Float charge: Gives reduced voltage and low current to keep it near fully charged without damage.

You can get multi-stage charges with even more levels, but the rough idea is the same.

How big a battery charger do you need?

Remember that a battery needs a charger with an output of at least 10% of the battery's capacity. For example, a 100Ah battery will need at least a 10 amp charger. Any less will reduce the capacity and it will take even longer to charge.

The bigger the charger (16A instead of 10A), the quicker it will charge up your battery. If you remember our earlier example about needing to replace 50% of a 100A battery, a 16A charger would do it in just over 3 hours, whereas a 10A one would need 5h.

Checking a battery's charge level

Many motorhome leisure batteries have a light or display to show the charge level. They may not be 100% accurate, but it will give you a rough idea.

A hand-held unit is generally more accurate, but unnecessary in most situations. If you use a hand-held meter, 12.7+v means fully charged, while 12v or below means discharged. 12.4v is about 50%.

You can also use a hydrometer to measure the electrolytes in the cells. The reading should be between 1.1 (discharged) and 1.28 (fully charged).

Before a reading, turn off all electrical appliances, including alarms, fridges and clocks that run off the battery. Failure to do so will result in an inaccurate reading.

Also, do not do a test for 4 hours after driving or using a battery charger; a recently used battery will give a higher reading.

Safe handling of a Lead Acid battery

Batteries can be dangerous. If it ignites, it can cause burns or severe injuries and even explode. Lead-acid is also corrosive. Before you go anywhere near your lead-acid battery, do the following:

- Wear appropriate protective clothing, gloves and eyewear. Be warned: the acid can damage clothing if it gets on them
- Always remove the negative terminal first when disconnecting a battery
- Never smoke or have a naked flame near a battery
- Sparks can sometimes occur when connecting a battery. Use good quality clamps. Many

battery chargers are supplied with temporary crocodile clips; these are not suitable for permanent connections and should be replaced.

Gas

Pretty much every motorhome or campervan has space to carry at least one, but usually two, gas bottles. It's likely that your motorhome won't have one in it when you purchase it.

Gas is used for cooking, heating and power for things like the fridge when you're not plugged into mains electric. We use the gas as much as possible when not on mains as it saves battery power.

There are two types of gas bottle systems: exchangeable or refillable and there is two types of gas, butane (which is generally in a blue bottle) and propane (which is generally in a red bottle).

Exchangeable bottles are easy to get- just pop to anywhere which sells gas bottles (garages, bigger supermarkets, garden centres), ask them for a gas bottle (make sure it fits into your locker), sign the paperwork, pay the deposit and you'll be able to take one away with you.

Once that's done, you can return to that place and exchange the empty bottle for a full one (for a charge, obviously.) You cannot legally refill exchangeable gas bottles.

Refillable bottles - to use refillable bottles, most systems require you to buy and fit a dedicated refillable gas system and then you must visit a garage which sells LPG gas (yep, the same stuff used for LPG cars) to fill it. Those that don't, use the same connections and hose (pigtail) as the standard bottle swap system.

NOTE: If you fit a refillable system, you must tell your insurer, who will probably require you to get it checked by a professional.

Depending on your motorhome model, you may be able to drive with or without the gas being switched on. If you DO drive with the gas on (many people do if there are passengers in the back and they need the heating on), then please make sure you have anti-crash cut off and safety hoses fitted by an authorised gas fitter.

If you don't drive with the gas on (which is the safest option), then you need to remember to turn the gas system on when you stop before you can use it. Also, remember that to light your oven or hob, you'll usually need power for the electric ignition, unless you use a separate lighter.

We highly recommend getting a 3-way fridge which runs on gas, battery and mains; you'll find it a lot easier to manage power. (For clarity, it doesn't run on all 3 at the same time, but it is capable of using any of the 3 systems as needed.) Fridges will usually only run on battery when the engine is running!

Are exchangeable or refillable bottles better?

On one of our very first trips to Europe, we forgot to get new exchangeable gas bottles before we left the UK. We ended up in France with one completely empty bottle and one which ran out halfway through the night (we were there in March and it was so cold).

It was then that we discovered that an exchangeable gas bottle bought in France (or nearly anywhere on mainland Europe) will NOT fit directly onto your UK gas system. The fittings are different. You need a new 'pigtail' (hose) with a different connector.

Not only that, to get exchangeable bottles in France, you also need to fill in all the paperwork and pay the deposit for the bottle, which would end up costing a lot of money as you travelled around- you'd need to pay a new deposit each time.

For this reason, we highly recommend fitting refillable gas bottles if you're planning to do a lot of touring in Europe. Refillable gas is cheap and fairly easy to find nearly everywhere in Europe and we've easily saved what it cost to put in the system.

However, refillable gas is not always easy to find in the UK, so if you're planning to spend most of your time in the UK, you might prefer to save your money and stick to exchangeable bottles.

NOTE: It is possible to fit a fitted gas tank (underslung – under the van) instead of refillable bottles. However, having a tank fitted may prohibit you from being able to use the Channel Tunnel with your motorhome, even if the tank is closed off, so we don't recommend fitting one for that reason.

But you CAN use the Channel Tunnel with refillable or exchangeable gas bottles. You will also need to turn them off, which means the fridge will be off, but it's only for 30 minutes or so.

How much gas will you use?

A common question for new motorhomers is how much gas do you need? The answer (as with many things!) is… it depends. Your gas usage depends on when you are travelling, what you use gas for and how often you use it.

We spent 12 days touring Italy in July. We carried 2 x 6kg gas bottles and used just over one bottle in that entire time period. Because it was warm, we didn't use gas for heating- just for cooking and occasionally the fridge when we stayed on an Aire / Sosta. In summer, we usually say 6kg will do a week easily, even with a gas kettle which is on almost constantly- we're big caffeine drinkers!

However, in winter, one 6kg bottle will only last about 3 or 4 days, because we use it for heating and the heating is on almost all the time. If we travel with our daughter, who sits in the back, we have the heating on even when we're driving.

However, if your heating can be run from electric (some heating systems only run off gas), and you are staying on a campsite with hook-up, you won't need to use gas for your heating, which means your 6kg bottle will last longer.

We've found that the heating doesn't get as warm when using electric as it does on gas, so bear that in mind when selecting the temperature.

As you can see, there really isn't a definitive answer- make sure you have options. If you have exchangeable bottles, try to exchange each one as it runs out, rather than waiting to do both at once- Murphy's Law states the gas will ALWAYS run out in the middle of the night, when it's freezing cold… and you wish you had a new bottle to connect!

Motorhome Control Unit

Most motorhomes and campers have a central control unit- usually near or above the habitation door.

This unit allows you to turn on power for lights, water, heating and usually allows you to monitor levels for battery, waste and water, plus choose what power source you want to use for things like heating- battery, mains or gas.

There are many different makes and models of control units, so I highly encourage you to get your manual out and spend some time getting to know your unit, going through all the settings until you understand what they all do. Pay particular attention to how to turn the lights on and off- you'll use that button ALL THE TIME in the dark and knowing where it is when you first enter the van is really useful.

Don't be scared to play- there's not a lot you can do which will break the unit; they're pretty forgiving. One of the biggest mistakes we make (yes, even now), is turning the heating to gas… and then forgetting to turn the actual gas bottle on outside in the locker. Which causes an error code on the control unit. Doh.

Also, if you select electric for the heating, that doesn't mean you can't still use the gas for cooking or to run the fridge. You usually select the power source for the fridge inside the actual fridge itself and you can ALWAYS use gas for your hob or oven if it's a gas cooker.

Just remember to turn on the bottles outside. Oh, and if you have an electric lighter on the oven / hob, this won't work unless the power is switched on, but you can still use a lighter to light the hob / oven if you wish.

Solar Power

We love solar power. Even though we spend a lot of time exploring the UK, it's still been worth it for us to install a solar panel on every motorhome (and boat!) we've had.

The extra boost for the battery allows us to stay off-grid longer and also helps keep the battery a little healthier if we're not using it for a while.

Again, if you're ONLY planning to stay on campsites with electric hook-up, there's no need to get a solar panel, but if you're considering the odd night or two off-grid, or staying in an aire in Europe, or just want to stay in a campsite field without hook-up, you'll probably want to consider a solar panel.

This will depend on how good your leisure battery is and how long it will last based on your daily power consumption, so you may get a couple of days power without solar.

Although there are many options to buy a panel in cheap online places such as Amazon, unless you are confident with electrical systems, we highly recommend getting a professional to fit your solar panel and hook it up to your van.

Types of Solar Panels

Solar panels come in two main types: monocrystalline and polycrystalline. The major difference between the two varieties is size – a poly panel will typically be about 5% larger than a mono for the same quoted output.

Solar panels can be rigid or flexible- for vans we recommend rigid as they are more reliable and don't often need to be walked on (not many motorhomes have roofs strong enough to walk on!).

How big a solar panel do you need?

The answer to this has nothing to do with the size of your motorhome leisure battery. It has to do with how much energy you plan to use.

A small campervan with only a few LED lights will need MUCH less than an 8m motorhome with a fridge, heating, a 12v TV and lots of electrical devices to charge.

The most common size of solar panel is 80-100W. Ours is 100W and it's been fine on both a 7.8m motorhome with 2 leisure batteries and a 6.7m motorhome with only one. (No, we didn't remove the panel when selling- we just got another one of the same make fitted).

Be warned: solar panels are rarely as effective as they say they are. As an example, a 100W panel could technically (on paper) produce around 8A, but in reality, it's rarely that good- five or six amps is more realistic. On cloudy days it will produce even less.

Solar Power Regulator

If you have a solar panel, you will need a regulator to control the charge going into the battery. A typical solar panel in full sunlight could produce around 22 volts, which is too high for a 12-volt battery. The job of the regulator is to reduce this to a safe charging level so you don't damage your battery.

There are many different solar regulators available. Cheaper options include simple split charge or basic fixed voltage charging systems; multi-stage charging is better if you can- this reduces the charge as the voltage increases.

Some electrical units (such as Sargent) are able to take the power from the solar unit and charge up both the leisure and engine batteries as required. These systems often have a maximum solar wattage that they can handle, so ensure that the panel you choose does not exceed it.

We recommend ALWAYS getting your solar panel professionally fitted- if you get it wrong it's no good to you and is just a heavy lump. It could even cause damage to your battery or electrical system if you really get it wrong. Again, you might need to declare this to your insurer once it's fitted.

Generators / Power-banks

I'm a firm believer that if you are planning to spend most of your time on a campsite, you do NOT need a generator in your motorhome. Save your money and the weight for something more useful.

Having said that, if you want to spend as much time as possible off-grid (as we do), you might find a generator useful, even if you don't use it very often.

I think we used ours about 6 times over 3 years- but we were grateful for it each time!

We mainly used a generator to charge our electrical devices when we've been off-grid for a few days (and are not driving anywhere).

If you decide that a generator is something you're interested in buying, there's a whole section on how to choose the best type of generator for you in the 'Life on the Road' section.

Power-banks

Instead of a generator, we now carry a power-bank. These things are smaller and easier to handle than a generator and have made life off-grid even easier.

At the time of writing, there are 3 main players on the market- Jackery, Ecoflow and PowerOak- although more are being designed all the time.

We have both the Jackery and the Ecoflow. Both have pros and cons. You can read in-depth reviews of each on the Wandering Bird website but I would highly recommend one of them instead of a generator for most motorhomers who want to stay away from hook-up.

Water

The water system in your motorhome is a very basic version of the one in your house.

Firstly, you need to put water into the motorhome, usually done by a filler port on the outside (double check to make sure you're definitely putting water into the water tank- not the fuel! TIP- the fuel filler is by the engine; the water is usually further back).

Even if you don't plan to use the water onboard for drinking, it's worth always making sure to put fresh, drinkable water into the tank- just in case.

If you've not used the van for a while or if it's new, give the tanks a good clean- there are several solutions you can get which you just pour into the water tank (once you've added in water), leave overnight and then drain in an appropriate place. There's more information on these in the cleaning section, Part 7.

Once you've filled the tank, you'll need to turn on the water system in order to activate the water pump (check your pump is turned on at the control panel if your system is set up this way), which will pump the water from the tank up to the taps in both the kitchen and bathroom if you have one.

Note: Make sure the water release valve is closed. If it is open and you follow the below steps, water just pours out from the under the van via the release / empty valve. If you don't know what the valve is, this the switch next to or on your boiler that you open to release all water from the system when preparing for storage of your van.

It might take a few moments for the water to come through the first time and it may be a bit 'spluttery' *(another technical term!).*

Make sure the tap is turned to cold first, wait until the water comes through smoothly, then turn to hot. It will take a little longer for hot, as the water needs to fill up the hot water tank first (usually around 7litres or so), and then it will be pushed up to the tap.

Again, do this for both kitchen and bathroom sink and shower (although there's only one boiler tank to fill, so the second ones will be quicker.)

A common question we get asked is can you use the heating even if there is no water in the system? The answer is yes- just make sure the hot water boiler is switched off and it will all be fine.

Waste

There are two types of waste in your van- grey and black.

Grey is dirty water from your sink or shower and is collected in a tank, usually found underneath your van.

Black is toilet waste (also known as chemical waste), usually collected in a cassette directly under your toilet- you need to open up the toilet each time you use it- there should be a lever on the side to do this.

We'll cover emptying grey waste, toilet, plus using the heating, fridge, cooking and other things for living in your van under the 'first trip' section in Part 5.

PART 3- PACKING YOUR VAN

Before you set off on your first trip, you'll need to put at least some of the basics into your van. If you're only going for a night, we recommend just adding the bare minimum; if you're trying to find a problem or source of a leak, you don't need to be emptying out all your lockers to get to it!

However, our very first ever motorhome trip was a 300-mile trip to Wales, so I can't sit here and judge you for wanting to go on a proper adventure. Just know that we highly recommend spending at least the first night on a campsite near to your home to make sure everything works before you disappear over the horizon!

The first step is knowing what you need to pack. Obviously, this includes both inside and outside gear, so be prepared for lots of lists! Remember, not everything will apply to you or be possible on your payload- you need to make the final decision on what makes the final cut!

How to Pack a Motorhome

There are a million ways to outfit a motorhome for road trips and none of them are right or wrong. These are the steps I took to make sure I had everything we needed for our trips.

The first thing to do is assess your lockers. You will find that you have 'good lockers' and 'bad lockers' inside your camper. Good lockers are easy to access, easy to see inside and easy to keep organised. Bad lockers are hard to access / hard to see inside and large enough for things to get thrown in without any thought whatsoever, which makes them impossible to keep tidy!

Bad lockers may also have heating duct pipes / wires / switches etc inside them, which means you need to think about the types of objects you put into them, so that you don't squish / damage the pipes.

Putting things away

Your first job is to gather together all the things you want to pack into your van. If you have it, a spare room or garage is invaluable for this, so you can buy and store things easily without cluttering up the rest of your house. Try not to add things to the van 'willy-nilly'- you'll lose track of what you've already put onboard and end up with way more than you need.

Don't panic- I know it can look like utter chaos once everything is gathered, but we will get through this very quickly and it will start to feel a lot more under control. You might find it helpful to store things in orderly piles in your spare room / garage so you can find things for the same area quickly, like tools, kitchen gear or bedding.

TOP TIP: Do yourself a favour- send the kids, dogs (and possibly spouse!) out for an ice cream or a loooooooooooooong walk. It will take half the time if you can just concentrate and work through it methodically.

Start by identifying your good / bad lockers, then get started putting things away.

Tips and tricks for packing

Start with your heavy / awkward kit (Generators, outdoor furniture, tables, snow chains etc) If you have a garage or outdoor storage, this might be fairly easy, but for many motorhomes, it requires thinking about your lockers carefully

Put things that you don't expect to use very often, like generators or snow chains, in the 'bad / annoying to get to places', like under the bed or in the middle of the garage etc. Save the good spaces for things you want regular access to

Put heavy items as low as possible

Also, consider your weight distribution. You don't want to put all the heavy things at the back or in the garage. Many motorhomes are front-wheel drive, so loading up the rear axle is dangerous - not to mention you'll probably bust the rear-axle weight allowance. (You can find your rear axle weight out at the weighbridge.) You want the weight spread over each axle as evenly as possible

Next, gather up all your kitchenware, crockery, utensils and plates etc. Try to put them in places which make sense but keep things secure. Don't forget to allocate space for tinned, dry foods, and for constantly used things, like coffee, tea and Custard Creams ;)

TOP TIP: Try not to carry many extra plates, mugs and glasses. We carry 3 of everything- and a couple of spare stackable mugs. That's it.

Store tins & heavy things which could roll as low as possible and put them in bags or boxes to stop them moving around.

Protect your heating ducts inside the lockers. You don't want to store any perishable food next to these pipes, as they will get hot. You also don't want heavy items to fall inside a cupboard or locker and squash the duct or damage a pipe- that can be an expensive repair and leave you without heating or some other issue.

Allocate easy-access space for tools, electric cable, spares and chocks; all the things you need on a regular basis.

Then move on to clothes and personal items. Bathroom stuff and toiletries is fairly easy- you might find some plastic boxes useful to keep things dry and easy to find.

What to pack

As I've said several times already- it's VERY easy to overpack. Sadly, it's not as easy as just stopping when the lockers are full- you can easily have empty lockers and STILL be over your maximum weight.

Don't forget, you don't need EVERYTHING that you have in a house. In fact, how you live in a house is unlikely to be how you live in a motorhome, especially if you're using the van for holidays instead of a permanent lifestyle.

It's unlikely you're going to spend your holiday time cooking full Sunday roasts or baking bread and cakes (although I know some people do- personally I prefer to visit the local pub and be spared the washing up!!)

Everyone is different and over time you will learn how you use the van and the sorts of activities you enjoy doing. Don't be afraid to remove things you haven't used for a while and don't worry about 'what if: if you suddenly get an urge to bake a cake and find you don't have a cake tin onboard, you can pick one up very cheaply from the local supermarket. You don't have the payload to carry EVERYTHING with you.

Don't forget to make space for hobbies as well. We are motorbikers, so we need to carry all our leathers, helmets, and boots etc. If you enjoy surfing, paddle boarding, or have kids, dogs or other pets, you'll also need to add on extras.

Once you have a list of things, you might want to weigh each item and keep a running total of what goes on board, so you can keep an eye on your payload. We didn't do this for EVERYTHING, but we did for the bigger items.

To do this, literally stand on a bathroom scale, take note of your weight without any items, then stand back on holding something and note what the difference is. It's worth keeping this list so you can calculate the difference if you choose to remove that item later.

Alternatively, you can use a set of hand-held luggage scales, where you can get the weight of the item just by hooking it onto the scales.

But the easiest and most precise method is to go to the weighbridge when you're packed and see how you did- I guarantee almost everyone goes overweight the first time! I know we certainly were.

NOTE: If you suspect you might be overweight, take a friend with a car with you so you can offload some gear in order to legally drive home again. Or get any passengers to walk back…

Outside / basic motorhome gear

Here's a list of useful things every motorhome or camper needs. If you need to buy any kit, you can find everything we recommend in the Wandering Bird Amazon shop: https://www.amazon.co.uk/shop/wanderingbirdadventur es

Hosepipe

You will need a hosepipe to fill your water tanks. We highly recommend getting one at least 10-15 metres in length. **A food grade hose is preferable** as it won't degrade and get bits in your water tank. We prefer a proper hose but a flat hose is a lot easier to store.

You will also need connectors- we like the Hose-lock connector and use brass adaptors for Europe for different size taps.

230/240v Electric cable

A long (25m) electric cable is good. Make sure it was one two ends with round connectors- one end (with flap) goes into your van and one goes into the electric bollard on the campsite.

Don't leave it coiled up when in use as it could cause a fire. We prefer not to have it on a reel as it's easier for stowage and also means we don't get lazy and leave it coiled up on the reel.

It is handy to get a connector to plug into a domestic plug in the event you park up on your driveway or visit friends. family while you are away.

Levelling chocks

You'll only spend one night at a weird angle before you agree that levelling chocks are a must. We highly recommend getting 'Jumbo' size ones– they take up a bit more storage room, but they're so much more useful than the smaller versions. A storage bag is useful too for when they're wet and / or muddy from a field.

Mud Mats

Talking of mud, have you ever been stuck on a muddy pitch or field with your camper? We have… and it was NOT fun.

I don't think we would have gotten out if it wasn't for these mud mats. You might not need them often, but when you do, you REALLY do!

Motorhome Wing-mirror protectors

These are one of the best things you will ever buy. Trust me- worth every penny. There are long arm and short arm versions- be sure to buy the correct one for your motorhome or camper.

They just clip over the existing motorhome or camper wing mirrors (I say 'clip on', you may need to give them a forceful push) and stop them being damaged if you scrape a wall or someone coming the other way is too far onto your side.

Safety Kit

If you have got gas onboard, you need a carbon monoxide detector. And a smoke alarm. A fire blanket and fire extinguisher are also important- put them somewhere easy to reach, like near the habitation door.

Other essential safety kit includes:

- Spare bulb kit and fuses of various sizes.
- First Aid Kit
- Warning Triangle
- Basic toolkit
- Head torch / normal torch and spare batteries.

If you are heading to Europe, you will need some additional safety gear which you are legally required to carry. You can grab a FREE checklist of all this kit here >>>>

Tyre Repair Kit

Many motorhomes do NOT have the ability to carry a spare wheel - they have a tyre repair kit. Make sure it's a heavy-duty system suitable for large vehicles and be sure to keep it in date.

Interior Accessories

There are several things you'll need inside your motorhome, even if just for one night. You can find what we currently use at wandering-bird.com/mms

Toilet Paper & Toilet chemicals

You do NOT need expensive 'motorhome' toilet paper. In fact, the cheapest stuff you can find in the supermarket is perfect- anything which dissolves quickly.

But you will need proper toilet chemicals. We've tried a lot of different types, including detergent tabs, which were ok but didn't stop the smell.

Also, if it's a 'new' van to you, you might want to freshen up the toilet cassette.

Bedding & mattress topper

Decent motorhome bedding is essential. We aren't a fan of sleeping bags, preferring proper duvets and pillows. Don't forget you'll need sheets as well.

A mattress topper is also useful if you want a good night's sleep, especially if you're not on a proper mattress but a 'put-together' bed from cushions.

Cleaning Gear

If you spend much time in the motorhome, it's going to need cleaning. We have tried several different brands of 12v vacuum cleaner and conclude that Dyson is worth every penny. Get the one with a 12v charging option. You'll also want a small dustpan and brush to get in the corners. You'll also need kitchen roll, wipes or spray and cloth and washing up kit.

Kitchen Basics

Once the heavy and awkward stuff is stowed away safely, start looking at food. We don't do a lot of fancy cooking in our motorhome, but we like to keep the basics like flour / sugar etc in airtight sealed boxes. We find it makes them last longer and stops any little insects getting in.

Try and keep 1-2 rolls of paper kitchen towels easily accessible but store the rest in lockers under the seats. You don't want to take up all the good lockers with things like paper towels or toilet rolls, which you only need to access every few days.

Make sure sharp knives and other kitchen tools are safely stowed. We used to put ours in a drawer, wrapped in soft cloths so they can't accidentally cut anyone, but now we have a magnetic knife strip on the wall, which we use. We'll put knives away for long trips, but otherwise we leave them on the strip.

We don't recommend carrying many extras for mugs, plates and cutlery. If there are only going to be 2 of you in the van, there's no need to carry 6 place settings. We carry a couple of spare mugs, and one extra plate / bowl / cutlery set.

If we meet people out on the road and want to share a drink or a meal, they'll have their own glasses / plates on their van, or we do a mash-up of whatever we can find. It's easily fixed for the few times it happens and not worth wasting storage space for.

The basic kitchen essentials include:

- Plates & bowls
- Mugs & glasses / cups
- Cutlery
- Condiments
- Spatula / wooden spoon / stirrer / tongs, tin opener & bottle opener
- Sharp knives, including bread knife
- Tea towels & washing up stuff
- Bin bags (doesn't have to be the big black ones- we find the smaller pedal bin size are often better and fit in the motorhome bin on the door).
- Kitchen roll
- Frying pan / saucepan
- Oven tray x 2
- Gas / non-electric kettle

We also find the following useful to have onboard:

- Plastic boxes in the fridge to hold things in place
- Bottle bag (one of the wine carrying ones from a supermarket- these hold bottles and stop them clinking together).
- Oven mitt
- Dish-drying matt (we don't use a rack- takes up too much space).
- Poach-pods (have I mentioned I love poached eggs? These things are a brilliant invention).
- Chopping board (two max).
- Steak knives- if you're partial to red meat.
- Soup spoons (if you eat (drink?) soup!).
- Don't forget things like tea / coffee / sugar / hot chocolate and food!

Personal Items & Clothes

By now, most of the lockers will be filling up, especially the ones under the motorhome seats. It's time to think about clothes.

Try to split your clothes into things you'll want daily (underwear, socks & t-shirts etc) and things you might not use every week (snow gear, hiking boots & bikini etc) Obviously, this will depend entirely on where you are road tripping and what you enjoy doing there!

We tend to store shoes and boots for outdoor and water activities in a separate locker or box under the table. We hang clothes in the wardrobe, and we have one small cupboard each. Coats get either hung in the bathroom or put on the drop-down bed when dry (we use the drop-down bed as an attic, not a bed).

If you are only travelling in your camper for a short period, then pack according to the weather.

TOP TIP: Always bring a jacket / fleece / warm jumper, even if the forecast is perfect. You'd be amazed how many times we've been caught out! Besides, even sitting out by a campfire can get chilly as it gets later. If you'd like to treat yourself, we have a range of van-life hoodies and zip ups on the Wandering Bird website.

Here's a list of things we keep or have kept in the van, to help you create your own list: (it's a baking hot day as I write this, so beach stuff is coming up first!!)

- Swimming gear / bikini, goggles
- If you're going somewhere beachy, a lightweight coverup for the beach which protects arms / shoulders if it gets too hot.
- Sunhat
- Scarf / shawl

- Fluffy socks (in place of slippers!)
- Pyjamas / sleepwear
- Sports Kit - leggings, t-shirts, socks, sports bra & phone holder
- Underwear, socks & tights
- Shorts, skirts & dresses
- Jeans
- Combats / lightweight trousers
- Joggers (For lounging, not exercise!)
- T-shirts / vest tops
- Hoodies, jumpers & cardigans
- Fleece for sitting around the campfire
- Warm hat, scarf & gloves
- Waterproof jacket / warm coat
- Jewellery if you're bringing it (ideally, leave it safely at home).
- Sunglasses
- Umbrella
- Walking shoes / boots / trainers
- Cheap sandals / flipflops for wearing to the toilets or at beach / lake which might get wet.
- Nice shoes for meal out
- Shampoo & Conditioner
- Body wash
- Shaving kit / razors
- Toothbrushes, toothpaste & mouthwash
- Deodorant / body spray / perfume
- Face cream / body lotion / hand cream
- Makeup
- Face & body wipes / face cloth
- Night cream
- Suntan lotion / Aftersun
- Antiseptic hand wash
- Hairbrush & hair bands
- Cotton buds / pads

- Contact lenses and/or glasses (including spare pair for drivers).
- Medicine (including contraception)
- Sanitary protection
- Dry shampoo
- Tweezers & nail-clippers
- Towels
- Beach towels & rugs for sitting on
- **Medication & First Aid**
- Paracetamol / Ibuprofen
- Antiseptic throat spray / lozenges
- Imodium
- Spray plaster
- Savlon wipes / cream
- Cough medicine
- Vaporub
- Antihistamine / Hayfever tablets
- Bug bite cream
- Insect Spray

Other items

It's time for the tools / 'bits'. We all have these, the things that go in that 'special' drawer in your kitchen at home. It's rare you'll be able to find a drawer in your motorhome just for this purpose (lucky you if you do!).

We have a 'bits box', which sits inside one of our cupboards and holds batteries, tape, string, playing cards, pens, notepad and a million more things.

Again, try and keep things you think you'll need frequently easily accessible, and put other things towards the bottom / back. Some 'bits' to remember are:

- Headphones / Portable speaker
- Portable Charger / USB charger
- Hard drive
- Wi-Fi Dongle
- Wallet (with driving licence)
- Small Bag, Beach bag / backpack
- Kindle /books
- Beach games, football or Boules
- Electronic games
- Portable DVD player or tablet (if downloading games / video- try to do it before you leave).
- Torch
- Spare batteries
- Games / cards or whatever you choose to do to relax.
- Chargers for phones / laptops / tablets / Wi-Fi / bike headsets / portable radios… you get the idea!
- Placemats / tablecloth if you wish. We don't use these indoors, but we do use a tablecloth if we're setting up a table outside.
- Cleaning gear. We keep cloths, duster, wet wipes and vanish spray all easily accessible.
- Bedding: Pillows, duvet, bedsheets etc. We have proper bedsheets- we're not a fan of sleeping bags. Remember, unless you have a fixed bed, you'll need to allocate somewhere to store the bedding during the day.
- Laundry stuff. Most laundrettes require you to provide your own detergent etc. We bring a small amount of ours so it's ready if we need it.
- COINS (in the local currency.) For parking, tips, tolls- you'll always need them!
- Camera gear / SD cards
- Water purification tablets

- Clothes Storage Hacks

Storing clothes in a motorhome makes me a little crazy. Seriously, the motorhome manufacturer states the van is built for 6 people... but you can't even hang 6 coats up in the wardrobe, let alone any other clothes!

I'll be honest, despite being ex-military and living on a boat for years, I found packing our clothes for long-term motorhome travel tough. I had far too many clothes and there just wasn't enough room to store them all!

Because we travel all over Europe in our motorhome, we need clothes for hot summer days, clothes for cold winter hikes (or impromptu trips up into the mountains), walking clothes, exercise clothes, smart clothes, casual clothes and clothes for when you're feeling bloated and nothing else fits.

(Tell me I'm not the only one who has days like that…)

To make matters worse, every single one of those outfits requires different shoes! And that's before we even get started on Mr WB's stuff…

However, over time (and whilst trying to hide clothes from my husband!) I've found some great storage places for clothes. 😊

Sadly, don't forget that clothes are counted in your payload too, no matter how well you hide them! Here are some of our favourite clothes storage tips:

Hide clothes in cushion covers

This idea is so simple. Just remove the stuffing pads from your throw cushions and put soft clothes inside instead. Ideally, it works better for things you don't need to iron.

I have two throw cushions which store warm snuggly blankets, another one which has winter gear such as hats, scarves and gloves, and one for gym gear and tights. We haven't gone as far as getting rid of our pillows yet… but I guess you could do that too!

TOP TIP– pack the cushion quite tightly so it keeps its shape. Nothing worse than a saggy cushion. Also, try to get a cushion with a zip on the back- you don't want things falling out if someone moves it!

Admittedly, if you want to use the blanket or haven't done washing in a while, the cushion will be empty for a while, but for us it's a good trade off.

Use mesh bags for underwear and socks

Mesh bags are brilliant because you can see into them, and they fit into any space available. They're also a great way to keep underwear and socks neatly organised and not falling about inside the cupboard.

Get bags with a zip to make it easy to store. We have several of these in various sizes for underwear, socks, dog toys and loads of other things.

I like using the ones designed for travel on airplanes as they can compress down easily.

Alternatively, you can buy compression/ vacuum storage bags which come with a pump you can use to squish down bulky clothing or bedding into easier to store packages.

Put boxes on the wardrobe floor and in shelves

Boxes are perfect for storing bulky things like jumpers, t-shirts and jeans, which take up a lot of room inside a small wardrobe. We try to stack things 'on end' so you can easily see what's in the box.

I prefer to keep our boxes removable, so we can pull them out to see the contents, but you can always put a screw through the bottom into the wardrobe base to keep it in place. Make sure the box fits securely, so it doesn't move / bang around.

Put storage on the back of the bathroom door or any door!

We love a good soft hanging storage set. This is a simple idea which we've used on the boat for years. We've tried a selection of them over the years and my favourites are the ones without zips... because I'm lazy and I never zipped them up anyway! They're brilliant for storing shoes, bottles, knick-knacks, makeup, belts and a million other things.

Screw them to the door (be careful not to use long screws which will go through!!) and that way they won't rattle around when you're driving.

Get a box for your shoes

Shoes are a pain to store in a van. Eventually, we got a collapsible box and now we store it under the table. (Get plastic bags for muddy boots!) If you need to use the table, put the box in the passenger footwell when you're parked, and move it when you're driving again. Easy-peasy.

If you want to be REALLY organised, get some large elastic bands and secure the shoes together in pairs so they're easy to find.

For this, I do recommend an easy to clean, plastic box. You'll be amazed how muddy it gets.

TOP TIP: DO NOT PUT CLOTHES AWAY WET- it will cause damp & condensation. We hang wet clothes in our bathroom to dry first. If you don't have a bathroom, hang some elastic over the front cab or any place you're not using and let things dry there before putting them away.

Packing your motorhome without rattles

We have a running joke in our van. We set off on a road trip… and 30 seconds later we stop again in order to go and fix something which is rattling or making noise. This is often repeated several (or many!) times at the start of each trip.

Some people can just turn up the radio and ignore the noise. That's me, but sadly, it's not my husband. Noises and rattles annoy him intensely and aggravate his tinnitus. You would not believe the number of times we've stopped in a layby or parking area and then tried to figure out where the mystery noise was coming from.

I swear, camper vans have their own special kind of 'rattle which can NEVER be found until you're driving! I have even gone so far as to sit in the back seats whilst we were travelling so I could hear for myself where the noises were coming from!! This is where learning how to pack a motorhome or camper properly can really help.

Some tips for reducing rattles in your motorhome include:

- The tighter you pack things into lockers and cupboards, the less space things will have to move around and the less noise they will make.
- Put breakable things somewhere secure. I know it sounds obvious but I'm the idiot who put our wine glasses on a shelf because "they look pretty". Not for long, they didn't! (*It's ok to keep things on a shelf whilst you're parked up- just remember to put them away again before travel).*
- Keep heavy items as low as possible in the van and forward if you have a front-wheel drive. i.e., put tins or the generator in a front locker if possible, not the back.
- Keep items you use regularly as accessible as possible. The more annoying it is to get to something, the more annoying life in a motorhome will be. Try to make things easy for yourself.
- Make sure clothes and shoes are stored securely. It's amazing how much noise these can make.
- Bathrooms are another easy-to-miss area. Keep bottles and toiletries packed tightly together.

Tips for packing your motorhome kitchen

You'll probably find the kitchen area is the worst culprit for rattles. There are just so many dishes, mugs, cutlery, pans, not to mention the oven, hob and microwave, it's a never-ending noise. If you can reduce the rattles enough during 'normal' driving conditions, you'll be doing well, but still expect the odd 'clink' on a particularly bumpy road.

Here are some tips on how to pack up your kitchen to help stop the noise:

Put a tea-towel or cloth into your cutlery drawer- on the top, so it's a tight fit when you push the drawer closed. This stops the cutlery 'jumping' and clinking together.

Similarly, put a layer of non-slip matting underneath the cutlery inside each section to stop them sliding.

Stack pots and pans inside each other and put a thick tea towel or a double layer of non-slip matting between pots and pans so they don't scratch or rattle. Try to stack the lids either inside or wrap them up in a separate layer of non-slip so they don't touch.

Stop plates rattling by putting large paper plates between them. Same for bowls.

Hanging mugs look pretty but they're going to make a lot of noise and possibly break whilst you're travelling. Put these away before you start driving. We bought some stackable mugs and put a layer of kitchen towel between each mug.

Separate any jars, spices, or bottles (including alcohol)-wrap them in non-slip or kitchen towel so they can't touch each other. It only needs to be a thin barrier.

Secure the oven shelf with flame-proof plastic strips-they are amazing for stopping the shelf 'jumping' in the oven as you travel. Alternatively, remove the shelf while travelling.

Remove the microwave plate and ring while driving- they create so much noise! Wrap them in a tea-towel or non-slip and store them in a locker or cupboard.

Put a tea-towel under the metal bit of the hob so it doesn't clink over each bump. DON'T do this until it's cool.

We also put a tea towel in the oven door to help stop the noise it makes.

Whilst we're talking about kitchens & food, here are some tips for packing tins & organising your cupboards:

Write the name and expiry dates of tinned foods on the top of the can (if storing in a low locker) so you can easily see what they are and what needs eating first.

Group similar types of food together. Put all tins of meat one side of the locker, vegetables at the other. You'll find it easier to plan a meal if you can see what you have left.

I try to stack the same thing on top of each other so I can find things easily. As the locker gets emptier, this gets harder- you also need to pack the locker so things don't fall or rattle around.

Write down the contents of your food lockers in a notepad and try to remember to cross off things as you use them. It helps me see easily what food we have onboard, which helps with meal planning and shopping.

Put 'naughty' sweets & treats in an inaccessible locker. It makes you REALLY want them to get them out. It works surprisingly well!

Motorhome door rattles

The doors on motorhomes are notorious for rattling. Sadly, there's often not a lot you can do to stop this. Try to make sure the door is secure in its fittings and all screws are tightened.

If the door itself feels loose, or if there is a draft, some draft excluder or foam strip around the edge will help create a better seal, which will also stop the motorhome door rattling.

Normally, the rattles are caused by the fixtures on the door rattling. Try adding a small piece of tape between the fixtures and the motorhome door, which might stop them hitting against each other as you're driving.

The other thing which causes a lot of noise on our van door is the flyscreen magnetic catch- and the bin. See if you can tape / secure them better.

Stop Windows rattling & reduce Motorhome wind noise

Another common culprit for camper van rattles are the windows. Again, make sure they are secure- it's amazing how quickly screws can work loose while you're traveling.

We have put a slim foam seal around each edge- it's also really helped keep the wind out and reduce motorhome wind noise while driving.

Overhead bed

Many modern motorhomes have a drop-down bed, either over the cab or over the forward seating area. These are AWFUL for noise- especially if they're on tracks. On both vans we've had with a drop-down bed, the tracks were loose and made a heck of a racket.

On our current van (Swift 685 Escape), the bed actually had a recall on it, so extra straps were added- which has helped reduce the noise too.

Our Swift 685 Escape in the middle of the French Pyrenees

PART 4- PLANNING A TRIP

Before you can set off on your first adventure, you need to know where you're going!

As with most things in motorhoming, you'll find that what works for one person isn't going to work for someone else. Some people can only travel during school holidays or during holidays from work, while others are retired but may have family commitments or may have as much time as they like.

Having said all that, the steps for planning a trip are the same for almost everyone, so we'll work through them together.

TOP TIP: We highly, highly, HIGHLY recommend booking a night or a weekend away somewhere close to your house for your first trip if you can't spend the night on your driveway.

I can guarantee that you will forget something and being close to home will make it possible to nip back and get it if you need to. It also makes things easier if you know the roads / can avoid low bridges etc.

Even if you like the idea of motorhome wild camping / staying off-grid, book into a campsite for the first night or two, while you can test out everything and make sure it all works ok. If you want to test how your van does 'off-grid', just unplug the electric cable while you try out all your systems at the campsite.

Deciding where to go

One of the hardest things about being able to go ANYWHERE is choosing where to go first.

NOTE: I am not taking into account any travel restrictions, laws or other regulations which may or may not be in place when you read this, as who knows what might happen in the future. Please do stay within any government rules or guidelines when planning your trip.

Here are a few questions to ask yourself about the sort of holiday you want to have:

- How long do you have for your trip?
- How long do you want to drive for?
- Are you happy to drive on motorways / toll roads (i.e.- you can go further, faster) or do you only want to drive on smaller / free roads (or a mix of the two?!)
- Do you want to see / do something specific?
- What sort of weather do you hope to enjoy? (Warmer or colder).
- Are you happy to go to a foreign country? Driving on the other side of the road, speaking a foreign language, eating foreign foods? Not everyone is, and that's ok. Better to figure that out now, rather than later!

Once you've answered those questions, you should have a rough idea on the area you can reach in your time frame- assuming you have a time frame of course!

For the purposes of this guide, let's pretend we have a week and we've decided we want to visit Scotland with our motorhome.

(If you ever do decide you want to visit Scotland, we've created a complete Scotland Road Trip planner, with guides to campsites, routes and more. Find out more on **www.wandering-bird.com/scotland**

Once you've decided on a rough area / destination, you need to start researching specific things to do / see once there. Literally, type into Google "Best things to do in_____ (in this case, Scotland or a specific place in Scotland)"

Invariably, millions of results will be returned, but everything you need will normally be on the first page or two of Google. Something like a TripAdvisor 'Best Sights' Board or a Tourist Information website is perfect to get you started to help you find places to visit and things to do.

The other place to look is Pinterest. Seriously, it's BRILLIANT for finding itineraries, ideas and cool places to see. If you'd like to see our itineraries on Pinterest, just search for Wandering Bird.

Whilst you're looking for places to visit, keep in mind your reason for visiting. There's no specific number of places you need to find, just educate yourself on the best things to do in that region so you don't miss out AND so you can start planning a route very soon.

Of course, if you are planning your trip for a specific reason, such as visiting friends or attending a wedding or event, then start there and work backwards, finding other things to do along the way if you have time.

Also, don't try to plan too much. If you only have a weekend, you're not going to see the top 100 sights in Scotland. Start narrowing down the ones which most appeal to you.

WHY are you visiting?

Another thing to bear in mind is WHY are you visiting wherever you're heading?

In our example, we're going to Scotland to explore the coastline and drive the NC500, see some history and castles, stand at John o'Groats and visit some whisky distilleries

For you, it might simply be as easy as "I've never been there before" or "I like the wine, food and weather, and I want to go back."

There doesn't need to be a serious and impressive reason to go anywhere. After all, it (hopefully!) isn't going to be your last motorhome or campervan trip – there'll be many more to enjoy.

WHEN is your motorhome trip?

When you are planning to travel can be just as important as WHERE.

I accept, not everyone has control over the when. Being forced to travel during school holidays is tough and far from ideal. If you can avoid that time period, I highly recommend it- campsites are busier and more expensive, traffic is worse, and attractions have longer queues.

However, if you don't have a choice, consider that you may need to book things further in advance and have a little less flexibility than you might enjoy outside of high season.

If you are going in the heart of July or August, it will be useful for you to decide at this stage the sort of motorhome holiday you want to have.

- Do you want to stay at a campsite which has loads of activities for the kids to do, or a beach / playground / kids club?
- Would you prefer an adult only campsite with a restaurant so you can relax and don't need to cook?
- Do you want to make it up as you go, wild camp in your motorhome and discover a new place each night?

The reason this is important to decide early is that the best motorhome campsites in both the UK and Europe get busy and booked up VERY early- especially the ones with a beach / pool / kid's club / surf school / good restaurants.

If you want to stay on a specific campsite for a week / two-week break, you need to pick your dates, pick your place, and book it asap.

If you're going to Europe, you'll also need to book up the ferry / tunnel too. If you'd like to know more about travelling to Europe with your motorhome, check out our Complete Guide to Motorhoming in Europe (more details in the appendices at the end of this book).

You also need to consider the weather in your plans. Winter in Scotland may be quieter, but it's not great for road tripping- there's likely to be constant rainfall and possibly even heavy snow. Similarly, if you have a dog or want cooler weather, don't head to the Costa del Sol in July.

Route Planning

Hopefully, your Google search will have created a list of places you want to go. These could be attractions, campsites, friends- anywhere you want to visit on your trip. Now, you need to create a route.

Personally, I like to plot all the places I want to visit into a Google Map, either on a laptop or my phone. I add all the Places of Interest in as I find them, and then I start to see a rough route and itinerary developing.

Google Maps is great because it's easy to use and keeps all your ideas organised so you can find them again, but you can just as easily use a paper map, a printout or even a list on the back of an envelope! Whatever works for you.

Once you've added places you want to go, use the map to see how far apart everywhere is. From there, you can estimate how long it might take to drive between them. I try to give us no more than 4 or 5 hours driving per day, although many people find that too much.

At least every 3 or 4 days we have a 'no driving' day. My husband currently does all the driving (his choice!) and it's not fair for him to constantly be at the wheel, so we make sure to allocate a day or two for relaxing (or catching up on work.) We have had to learn to slow down and enjoy the journey, rather than rushing to get somewhere as quickly as possible- motorhoming is not about speed, it's about slowing down and savouring the adventure.

Don't be too rigid in your Itinerary. Allow time for chilling in the van on a rainy day with a good book, or passing a sign for a market, or a place that you didn't even know existed and going to visit that.

Great- you're doing well!

You've decided on where, when, for how long and how you're going to get there.

Where to stay overnight

There are a couple of options for overnight stops for motorhomes in the UK:

- Campsites
- Approved overnight stopping points.
- Wild / off-grid camping

In Europe, they also have a system of places called Aires, but sadly we don't have many of them in the UK, although they are growing in numbers.

Campsites

There are many different types of campsites across the UK and Europe. Some are all-singing and dancing, with swimming pools, nightly entertainment, restaurants and more, while others are more basic (and usually cheaper!).

Finding a campsite: It's usually pretty easy to find a campsite near to you or near to where you are going, especially if you're a member of a club or have a book with various sites listed.

There are also many online options and ways to find campsites. Here are a few websites we use to find places:

- Pitchup.com
- UKcampsite.co.uk
- Park4night.com
- Searchforsites.co.uk

Don't forget, if you are a member of the Camping and Caravanning club or Caravan and Motorhome club, you can use their websites and member packs to help you find and book places.

We highly recommend being members of one club or the other (or both!) if you're UK based, although it's NOT a necessity. You can normally use their sites even if you're not a member, although you will pay more per night.

If you have multiple pets, make sure they are allowed at the site- some campsites restrict dogs to 2 max.

Types of pitch

You will often have a choice between a site with a grass or hardstanding pitch. Hardstanding is usually gravel, which is perfect in the winter (less muddy due to the rain).

You can also choose an electric or non-electric pitch, which means you have somewhere to hook your electric cable up to. I would suggest electric for your first trip, so you can make sure everything works as it should. But keep in mind that not all campsites have electric on them, so it's worth reading the facilities offered, so you don't arrive disappointed!

Some campsites offer 'fully serviced' pitches. The services differ, but always include electric hook-up and usually a water tap on the pitch and often a grey waste drain. To use this drain, you'll probably need a pipe which connects to your grey waste outlet in order to get the water to the drain, but it does mean you can leave the grey waste switch open in the van and it all flows straight down the drain.

These pitches are often more expensive than the other types and they're not essential, so don't worry if you can't find one.

To book a campsite, either book online or phone them. If you're a member of a club, they'll ask for the membership number. Most places ask for a small deposit to reserve your booking, with the rest paid on arrival. There's normally a time limit which you can cancel a booking without penalty- usually 72 hours before you arrive.

CS/CL sites

There are many smaller campsites around the UK called CS (Certified Sites) and CL (Certified Locations). These are usually run by farms / smallholdings and are affiliated by either the Camping and Caravan Club or Caravan and Motorhome Club. Being a member of either club gets you access to these sites.

These sites are small, normally 5 pitches only. Electric hook-up (EHU) is usually available, as is water and often (but not always) waste disposal.

There won't usually be a toilet block, play area or any other facilities- it's just a small campsite / approved place to park where you can stay for several nights if you wish (and book in advance). Prices usually cost between £10-

£15 / night on these types of sites. If we're going to use a campsite in the UK, we try to use these as much as possible as we prefer the quiet to noisier campsites.

Approved Overnight Parking

As well as campsites, there are also several types of approved overnight parking spots for motorhomes and campervans around the UK and Europe.

Sadly, the UK isn't quite as accommodating as Europe, and don't have the same level of motorhoming infrastructure, but there are still options for you.

If you'd rather not stay on a crowded campsite, but don't want to wild camp (or are in an area where you can't) a parking scheme might be for you.

Brit Stops

Brit Stops is a great scheme which connects businesses who are happy to let motorhomes and campervans use their car parks overnight, in return for you visiting and spending money at their establishment.

In the UK, this is mainly pubs (who are happy to let you stay if you buy a meal or a couple of drinks), but there are also some breweries, vineyards, farm shops, restaurants and other businesses.

If you're already planning to eat out, or you enjoy visiting local markets or businesses, this is a brilliant scheme for you to join. You pay an annual fee and receive a book with details for all the businesses taking part. You also get a card or sticker which you will need to show.

Some places like you to phone them in advance, but many are happy for you to turn up within working hours (details are in the book.)

Remember, these are just car parks, so there are rarely toilets, waste disposal, or other facilities, although you can sometimes find a water tap to refill with fresh water.

Many countries in Europe have a similar scheme with businesses which allow free overnight campervan parking. There are places such as vineyards, restaurants, farms, chateaux and even a snail farm in France!

Other parking schemes

There are also several other schemes which are coming to light more recently, including forestry schemes, local council parkups and sports facilities with lots of parking, offering to let motorhomes or campervans stay overnight for a small fee.

The only problem is finding out that they exist. Some are on the parking apps we use (see section on 'How to find Places' below), but many are found by word of mouth or in Facebook groups.

Our hope is that people will get better at sharing the information in a more structured manner in the future so it's easier to find and support schemes like these which makes motorhoming more flexible around the UK.

Aires in Europe

If you're used to UK motorhoming holidays, you might find the concept of Aires a bit strange. These are overnight motorhome and campervan (not caravans, sorry) parking places, provided and maintained by the local council.

They are called Aires in France, Spain and many other countries, Stellplatz in Germany and Sostas in Italy.

When we're touring Europe in our motorhome, we use Aires ALL. THE. TIME. They're a fantastic way to tour cheaply and without having to book campsites in advance. If you are planning a trip to Europe, you can find out more about aires on the Wandering Bird website.

Wild Camping with a motorhome / van

It's hard to explain what I love so much about wild camping with a motorhome; the freedom, the feeling of no-one else in the world knowing where you are. The night sky. The quiet. Being self-sufficient (with a bed and a fridge and wifi ☺). I just LOVE it. I'd rather wild camp than anything else.

Yet, I was not always like this. The idea used to intimidate me completely. Over the years, we've built our confidence and experience until we're totally comfortable being off-grid.

There is some 'discussion' in the van-life community that it should be called 'free parking' or 'off-grid' camping. Call it whatever makes you happy. I call it all three, which honestly, is probably incorrect of me.

There's a big difference between 'overnight parking' and 'camping'. Overnight parking is tolerated in many places, whereas 'camping' (getting outdoor furniture out, using a washing line, having a fire etc) is often banned and reported to the authorities.

Some places are much more tolerant than others-Scotland used to be fairly tolerant, (although that's sadly changing in recent times), whereas places in popular resorts or near busy beaches are often banned completely, as is wild van camping in National Parks.

Wild camping in France- such a gorgeous location

Here are some basic rules for wild camping / staying off-grid:

- Stay well away from areas where wild camping is prohibited.
- Stay away from private land and buildings unless you have the owner's permission.
- Arrive late in the day (late afternoon at earliest) and leave by mid-morning.
- In most places, do NOT light a fire or BBQ. At all.

- Don't put out tables / chairs / awnings. This is not a campsite (NOTE- we have used our outdoor chairs and BBQ a few times when we've been wild camping in the middle of nowhere. Use your judgement).
- Don't make loud noise / play loud music.
- Clear up ALL litter and waste.
- Watch children and pets and don't let them wander away- wild camping doesn't mean there is no-one else around.
- Be sensible about safety. Lock doors and windows before going to sleep (there's a whole section on security later in this guide).

SCAN ME

If wild camping is something you'd like to try but feel a bit intimidated by, you can grab your **free wild camping checklist on Wandering Bird** to get you started. >>>>

How to find overnight parking places in the UK & Europe

When we're touring, I use three apps or websites to find overnight motorhome parking spots, as mentioned above. Each app has pros and cons, and we use them for different things.

Park4night

The best place for finding overnight parking spots is **park4night.com.** This site is FREE to join & there is both an app and a website. Most of the users are European, so you'll find thousands of spots all over Europe (and much of the rest of the world too).

It lists a lot of aires, wild camping spots, car parks and approved motorhome overnight stops, which is useful if you need something with hardstanding and not too far off the main roads.

There is a small annual charge for complete access to all listings and this is well worth paying in my opinion.

Searchforsites

Another good app for UK users is **searchforsites.co.uk,** which we really like due to its ease of use and wide range of various options in the UK.

Again, there is both a website and an app and a small fee for full access and again, it's worth paying if you want to find alternative places in the UK or even just independent campsites which aren't club affiliated.

It also lists plenty of pubs, restaurants and independent places which allow overnight motorhome parking. These aren't necessarily Brit Stops, so you don't always need to be a Brit Stops member to use them.

Most places have photos and reviews, which we find helpful when picking a location. You can also add your own spots to the app if you find somewhere awesome and wish to share it.

Camper Contact

If you have a larger motorhome or RV, or are towing with your motorhome, **Camper Contact** is a great option as it allows you to narrow the search results by length or vehicle height.

As we spend most of our time pulling a trailer with motorbikes on it, it's really useful for us to know which overnight spots or aires won't be suitable for us (if we're too long or the access road is tight.) It also has several options which aren't listed on the other two apps.

Again, I tend to use the app more in Europe instead of the UK and it does have a charge for the year, but so far I've only used the free version, which has been sufficient.

Preparing your vehicle for your trip

Preparing your vehicle for your trip is important, even if you're just going for one night. If you've ever spent time broken down on the side of the road, you'll appreciate how a little time pre-trip can save you a lot of time later.

(Sadly, I'm not guaranteeing you will NEVER break down, but doing these checks can certainly help!)

NOTE: For the sake of ease, I'm writing this section as you would tackle it coming out of winter storage or a period of not being used (like lockdown!), so you can come back to this section again and again whenever you need to.

Paperwork checks

- Is your vehicle road legal? Do you have a valid MOT?
- Is your insurance in date and are you covered for where you're going? (especially if going to Europe).
- Is your driving licence / passport in date?
- If you SORN'd your vehicle over winter or a period of disuse, remember to un-SORN it and tax it.
- Check your breakdown cover is current if you have it- and keep the details to hand in the cab.
- If travelling overseas with a pet, make sure you have the appropriate paperwork.
- Remember to take all the essential paperwork with you, along with your passports if going overseas.

Outside Jobs

It doesn't make any difference whether you start with the inside or the outside jobs, or in what order you do these, so work through them however you see fit.

Engine Checks:

- Oil levels
- Brake fluid levels
- Screen wash level
- Ad Blue levels (if used)
- Check visual condition of engine bay- any obviously loose or damaged hoses?
- Remove debris and leaves from drainage holes
- Turn ignition on- are there any warning lights?
- Check all vehicle indicator, reverse, and brake lights are working, including tow bar if towing.

Tyre & Wheel Checks:

- Pressure (consult your manual for optimum tyre pressure. Could be anywhere between 40-80 psi).
- Condition (any sign of bulging, cracks or flat spots?)
- Brake pads, discs and wear

Spare Wheel:

- If you have a spare wheel, get it out and inspect its visual condition.
- If stored in a cage under the van, lubricate the cage so it doesn't seize.
- If you have a tyre repair kit, check it's in date and good condition.

Gas Locker checks:

- Check the levels of the gas bottle(s).

- Turn on system (you might need to prime it (using surge button) and / or press the anti-crash button if it's reset).
- Listen and smell for any sign of leaks- come back in a few minutes to recheck Remember LPG sinks, so get low to the ground.
- Check hoses for any obvious signs of damage or loosening.

Garage / Outside lockers:

If you have a garage or outside lockers, visually inspect them for signs or damp or leaks. This is also a good time to have a clear out and remove anything you THOUGHT you'd use but haven't!

Other Outdoor jobs:

- Remove outside fridge vents or other vents which you put on for winter.
- Check condition of windscreen wipers- replace if necessary.
- Apply coat of Rainex to windscreen.
- Wash and wax the van and clear off roof debris (more on that in the maintenance section.)
- Fill the freshwater tank if possible (remember to close any drain points you opened to drain the system for winter!) Then check for leaks under the van.

Inside jobs

Again, there's no particular order in which to do these. We like to do the tank cleaning / overnight jobs first, then move on to electrical stuff, but it's completely up to you.

Cleaning:

Rinse out your water tanks and sanitise overnight (Use something like Puriclean, which you use by filling your tank at least halfway, adding the powder (or tab) and leaving to sit for a few hours, ideally overnight. Then rinse THOROUGHLY (we rinse at least twice.)

Grey Waste tank. Exactly the same- fill and rinse. You can fill either via a dedicated access hatch or pour water with the cleaning solution in it down a sink (or both sinks, so it gets into the pipes.)

Clean the toilet cassette. Fill with water, add solution and leave to soak overnight.

Check and wipe down all lockers and cupboards. You're looking for rodents and insects, but also signs of damp, cracks, damage or anything else 'not right'.

You will probably want to do a full clean of sofas, seats and carpets. I recommend doing this last, after everything else, but if you're washing down seats allow plenty of time to try.

If you need to buy any cleaning kit, see what we recommend at wandering-bird.com/mms

Interior Systems Checks:

- Check your leisure battery is working- unplug your van from mains power and use some appliances to make sure the battery(s) is holding charge.
- Turn on 12v internal lights (and the one for outside the habitation door).
- Turn on the fridge- does it get cold?
- Clean fridge
- Turn on heating- does it get warm (you can do this even without water in your system).
- Turn on gas and light all burners, grill and oven. If you have an electric hob or microwave, check that too once you reconnect power.
- If you have water, turn on hot water system and check water gets hot (make sure you have the tap in the hot position!).
- If you have solar, ensure it's working, and the battery is charging (even if it's just a tiny amount on a cloudy day).
- Check the fuse box for any signs of damage or blown fuses.
- Check safety appliances- fire blanket and extinguisher- are they in date?
- Test and change batteries in smoke alarm and CO_2 detectors.
- Check TV is working if you have one and you can get a signal.
- Check your emergency kit- spare bulbs, fuses, torch, batteries, spare glasses and first aid kit.

Departure checks

It's getting exciting now. Your vehicle is prepped, packed and ready to go! If you're anything like me, you're always in an excited rush to leave and just get out on the road.

This is the point where I must confess that I left my passport in a printer once- and didn't remember it until 5 hours down the road! (Yes, we had to turn back. You can imagine my husband's joy…☹)

We also ended up in France, on Easter bank holiday weekend (when all shops were closed) with two empty gas bottles. (Technically, that wasn't just MY fault, but a departure checklist would have avoided those cold, miserable days and nights!)

So, learn from our mistakes. Take the time to work through your pre-departure checks for the van, yourself and your house before you leave.

Here's a run-through for you.

Exterior Checks:

- Are exterior lockers / garage closed and locked?
- Are gas bottles full, turned off (if not needed for heating**) and locked?
- Have you put your awning and outdoor furniture away (including retractable steps!)
- Have you unhooked your electric cable / water / waste?
- Is your generator off and away?
- Is your TV / satellite aerial down?

- Is your windscreen clean and thermal screen away?
- Is your bike rack / rear storage secure? (With red / white warning board properly fitted if needed?)
- If you're towing, is your trailer attached and locks / clamps removed?
- Have you checked trailer lights work?
- Are you on chocks / electric legs?
- Are the kids / dog / spouse on board?

NOTE: In many modern motorhomes, it is possible to use the gas whilst driving to provide heating to passengers sitting behind the cab. We've done this for our daughter on several trips and it uses a LOT of gas, but at least she was warm.

However, you can only do this if you have the appropriate hoses and anti-crash safety cut-off fitted. Many vans have it as standard; if not, you can get a professional to fit it for you.

If you don't have this, make sure your gas is safely off when you're driving.

Interior Checks:

Here's what you need to do inside your van before you set off:

- Make a hot drink for the road- then leave the hob to cool before putting any cloth on it to stop rattles.
- Are your windows / vents / hatches / sunroof closed? Including in the bathroom?

- Is the Habitation door closed and locked?
- Everything in the kitchen put away and rattle-proof?
- How about the oven shelf / hob / microwave plate?
- Fridge secure?
- Check the bathroom for anything loose-including if the toilet is closed.
- Double check bedroom, wardrobe or anywhere the kids have been.
- Are the kids / dog secure in their seats?
- Are you sure? They're sneaky…
- Put away the TV
- Are all cupboards closed and locked?
- Check the dashcam / rearview camera.
- Check your mirrors and driving position.
- Put route into sat-nav and get details to hand of your first stop.
- Remember to put your hot drink somewhere safe in the front, along with easy-to-eat snacks.
- Put anything on charge which needs charging as you drive (laptops, camera/drone batteries etc)- we use an inverter to do this.
- Put phones / iPads / headphones on charge
- Double check the dog / kids again…
- DO YOU HAVE ALL YOUR PAPERWORK? Including your passport…
- Have you got something easy to eat for dinner? Try to keep things simple for yourself or prepare something in advance which you can just heat up.

Then relax- you're ready to set off! Now the fun can really start!

If you would like a FREE printable version of these checklists, you can get them here >>>

The places you can go once you're all set up! This was in Slovenia- stunning part of the world.

PART 5- YOUR FIRST TRIP

It's time! Your first overnight adventure in your van. I hope you're excited.

Here's a step-by-step guide on what to do when you arrive at your first campsite. Some of this is a consolidation of what we've spoken about previously, but I wanted to include everything in a logical order so you could work through it.

Before you leave, make sure you know what the check-in time is for the campsite. Most campsite have a strict earliest arrival time (and will not budge on that!)

What to do when you arrive at the campsite

When you arrive, there will usually be a reception building where you need to check in and pay your balance on your booking. Often, there is also a clear sign saying where arriving motorhomes/ campers should pull in but, if not, try to pick a spot which doesn't block the entrance / exit.

Go into the reception and check-in. They will ask for your name, registration number, vehicle length and sometimes width of the motorhome too, so make sure you know those. If it's a club site, you'll be asked to provide your membership number and/or card.

Many campsites charge for the parking spot, and then charge for the number of people and animals onboard, so they will ask how many adults / children/pets etc you have onboard.

If you are in Europe, they will often ask to see / take a copy of or even keep a passport while you remain on site, but this is less common in the UK.

You will then normally be given a map of the campsite (which often has the site rules on the back) and they will either tell you which pitch to park on, or tell you to go and pick your own pitch. If you do this, you often need to go back and tell them where you are parked.

If you booked a pitch with electric hook-up (EHU), you might be given a key or card to put into the meter. You may also be given a code for the showers / toilets and for the entry / exit barrier if necessary.

How to pick a pitch or parking area

There is no right or wrong answer to this. I promise. No-one will be judging you (although they will watch you drive around and park up!) It's entirely personal preference where you choose to park.

We don't use campsite toilets or facilities very often, so we tend to park far far away from them. We park even further away from children's play areas, bars, restaurants or other communal (noisy!) areas.

If there's a small, secluded corner without many people in it, that's where we're heading! The only exception to this is if we might be able to get a sea view; we'll brave people for the chance of a pretty view out of the windows!

Of course, you may want to park next to the kids play area, or the shower block. In which case, pick a spot near there. On a busy weekend, you might not get much of a choice at all!

One other thing to look for is a flat pitch where possible. If you can avoid having to level the motorhome today, it will make your life so much easier.

Once you've picked your pitch or parking spot, either park up (and let reception know), or leave a pitch marker (a sign which says 'sorry, this pitch is taken', or leave your spouse behind to 'save your spot' whilst you go and fill up with water if you need to).

It's best to get water now, before you get settled. (More details on how to fill up shortly.) Of course, if you already have water, just park up.

How to park up on the pitch

Most of the time this is fairly easy. If it's a marked pitch, just make sure you're within the boundary. If it's an unmarked field, even easier.

However, some campsites are VERY strict when it comes to how you can park on a pitch. Many sites have a little white post on the pitch which one corner or other of your van must be next to. This can be tricky, especially when new, but take your time and accept it might take a few attempts to line the van up perfectly.

Campsites like this often prefer you to reverse in, which is fine but a pain if your habitation door or awning isn't on the side they feel is 'correct'. If this is the case with your van, ask them how they would like you to park.

Now, it's merely a case of manoeuvring that big white lump of plastic into the correct spot. People WILL watch.

Do not be embarrassed. Take your time. Remember your length and swinging room and go slowly.

If it helps, everyone else has had the same struggle and learning curve.

TOP TIP: Try not to shout at each other if you're with your partner or with friends / kids. Be patient and kind while you learn and figure this whole thing out, especially if one or both of you is a complete beginner.

We use hand signals, which comes from military training and sailing boats. I'll give Mr WB a 3,2,1 countdown to stop in the correct place, or turning signals if he needs to move over one way or the other.

A raised clenched fist doesn't mean I want to punch his lights out… *(although it occasionally does!)* but it means stop. Immediately. Then I walk to the driver window and explain, calmly and quietly, that he's about to wipe out a flower bed and he needs to pull forward and straighten up.

Many people find parking to be one of the most stressful parts of your motorhoming trip, because it's so hard to see behind you. Make good use of your reversing camera (if you don't have one, get one), go slowly, and don't forget the phrase: "**Sorry for what I said when we were parking the motorhome!**" ☺

Filling up with fresh water

If you don't have water onboard, it's easiest to get it before you park up (unless you have a fully serviced pitch.) There will probably be several drinking water filling spots (which is basically a tap) around the campsite. Some campsites even have taps on each pitch, but most don't.

Unlike caravans, you need to take your vehicle to the fill-up point, OR you can get a collapsible water container and walk back and forth several times. We use both methods, depending on the campsite and how far away the tap is!

If you drive to the water, just pull up into the motorhome facility parking area (being careful not to block the road) and connect your water hose. You will often need to provide your own tap connector. We always use our own hose instead of a site hose, as we know where it's been and what it's been used for!

Turn the tap on slowly (and make sure the water is actually coming out before you put it in your van- I can't tell you how many times we've been patiently waiting for the tank to fill up... only to realise nothing was coming through, due to a kink in the hose or some other issue.)

Once you have a full fresh-water tank, don't forget to fill your toilet flush with water too, if you have a separate one. Then head back to your pitch- you'll probably need to go around the one-way system.

We usually put some Aquasol into our water tank with each fill-up. It's totally odourless and tasteless and helps kill any bacteria which might be in the water source or the tank.

Levelling the motorhome

Despite your best efforts to choose a flat pitch, you might find you want to level the motorhome. Take a deep breath- this is another task which can get stressful, but I promise you can do it.

The first thing Is to decide which way you need to level. Some people get lovely and technical with spirit levels, but we tend to do it the old-fashioned way- we sit still and listen to what our body is telling us.

Think of the van as 4 corners- which corner needs to raise up for the vehicle to feel level? Remember which way you'll be sleeping- you want your head level or higher than your feet.

You generally only need two levelling chocks on a motorhome– one for each side. Normally, you would use them on the front wheels, but it is possible to use them on the rear ones or both on one side if that works; it will depend on the pitch and the slope you're trying to correct.

Obviously, the chocks will RAISE the van- so you want them on the side / end which is lower. When you get the chocks out, you'll see a flat side and a side with a ramp / steps (personally, we prefer the step version).

Place the flat side on the ground, right in front of the wheel you want to raise. We find it much easier to drive forwards on to them, although some people prefer to reverse. Just position the chocks right up next to the wheel and keep the tyres straight so you don't fall off the edge.

Then, drive forwards slowly onto them. It's a balance between enough power and too much. You might have to go back and forth several times to get the angle right. One chock might need to be closer to the wheel, while another is a little further away, so it doesn't rise so much. It will depend on the slope.

Be patient – eventually you'll get really good at this, but for now it's all new and confusing, so don't expect it to go perfectly straight away. We also use hand signals for this (as long as it's daylight!)

Plugging in Electric / water / waster

Once you're level on the pitch, you can start connecting your electric cables and services (if the pitch has them- not all pitches are serviced.)

Always plug the end of the electric cable into the motorhome first (don't worry- there's only one end which can fit in the van, and one which goes into the power outlet on the site. You can't get that wrong).

By plugging the van end in, and then connecting to the site, you aren't walking around with a live electric cable.

Sometimes, it can be tough to figure out which electric point you're supposed to use, especially if you're between two potential ones. Sometimes they're numbered, but often it's just a case of plugging in to whichever one works.

Talking of which, sometimes you need to go tell the reception which pitch you're on, so they can turn on the electric for you (that way people who haven't paid for electric can't just use it for free) and sometimes you need to flip the breaker switch or pay at the meter to turn the electric supply on. You might even need to turn the cable in the socket to start the supply- reception should have told you exactly what to do to get power.

Once your cable is plugged in, try not to leave the excess cable coiled up. There have been incidents of electric cables catching fire when they are left tightly coiled (something to do with heat build-up and resistance).

We try to flake ours down the length of the van, without causing a trip hazard or blocking any paths.

We know the electric is plugged in correctly by looking at our habitation control panel and seeing if the lightning symbol is on. If not, there's an issue somewhere.

If your van is brand new, you might need to turn on the master control unit (ours is a Sargent), although that should have been done for you.

Habitation Control Panel

Your next job is to check your habitation control panel, usually just above or next to the hab door.

This controls most of the systems for inside the motorhome; things like lights, heating, and water. It's also where you can see the battery / solar power and how full your water and grey waste tanks are (the toilet cassette usually has a light which comes on when it's full, although this can be found on the toilet itself.)

Once the electric cable is plugged in and the power is on, you might need to press a few switches on the control panel for things to work. On ours, we need to press a button to turn on the water pump, and several different ones to turn on the lights. Your manual will explain what you need to do.

The other thing to test is the 230v plug sockets. Once the electric is on, take an electrical device and plug it in to each socket to make sure the socket works ok.

Serviced Pitch

If you booked a serviced pitch with water, you can connect your hose to fill the tank and either leave it connected (but NOT turned on permanently- it will overflow), or put your hose away and bring it out whenever you need it.

Similarly, for waste, you can connect a pipe which leads from your grey waste tank to the drain. Very few pitches have black waste disposal on the pitch- there tends to be a communal emptying point.

Turning on the gas

Assuming your gas bottle is turned off, strapped up and connected correctly, all you need to do is open your gas locker and turn on the bottle when you're parked up on site. Make sure you turn on the bottle which is connected. If you have a system where both bottles are linked together, turn on both bottles.

All gas bottles have an 'open' and 'closed' arrow on the top. Usually you're turning 'lefty-loosy' to open. You might also need to press the surge button (near the open/close screw on the bottle) and / or press the anti-crash protector button, often found on the back wall where the bottle connects to the van.

There will always be a brief hiss and smell of gas when you turn the gas bottle on. If this doesn't fade or if it gets stronger within a couple of seconds, turn the bottle off IMMEDIATELY and don't light anything nearby.

Wait for the smell to fade (open windows and doors for ventilation), then slowly turn the bottle on halfway. If it still smells strongly of gas, turn it off and seek professional advice.

Don't forget to get gas in advance- you can't usually get it at a campsite.

Cooking

The oven, grill and hob normally all use gas only (unless you have an electric burner on one of the hob rings.) Therefore, you can't use them until the gas is switched on. Most cookers also have electric lighters- you'll need to turn the power on to use that.

If you haven't already tested them, light up the hob burners, the grill and the oven and make sure everything works. You'll often need to hold the starter in for a few seconds before they will stay lit.

We have a gas kettle (remember, you can't use an electric one unless you're plugged in to mains or you have a small 12v one), so now's the time to put it on and make a brew!

If you have an electric hob ring, test this when you're plugged into mains and make sure it works correctly.

Fridge

Hopefully, you already have a 3-way fridge in your van, which means it can run on mains, gas and 12v. For clarity, it will only use 12v when the engine is running; it draws too much power to use it just from the battery.

If you don't have a 3-way fridge, you might want to invest in one- they're brilliant.

Most 3-way fridges can automatically switch between power sources as they become available, but you can also select which one you want to use. If possible, set the fridge to use mains over gas; you'll use less gas and the fridge tends to get colder faster and stay colder on mains rather than gas. You select this on the fridge itself, not on the motorhome control panel.

If the fridge is selected to use mains, and you unplug the electric, it will auto switch to gas (assuming gas is switched on.) If not, a warning beep will sound to let you know that the fridge has no power (remember, it can't use the battery as a power source unless the engine is running.)

Heating

The heating can usually be run from either mains power or gas. If you get the choice, use mains; heating uses a lot of gas. You'll need to select which power source you want to use on the motorhome control panel. You can also set the temperature you want and a timer for heating there too.

NOTE: Unlike the fridge, the heating does not automatically switch between power sources. So, if it's running on mains and you unplug the cable, it won't automatically switch over to gas. It also probably won't even beep- you'll just get a warning triangle on the control panel, and it will stop working.

This is also true if you're using gas and it runs out in the middle of the night- you usually only know when you start to freeze!

You'll find that areas nearest the heater unit get the warmest, whilst those furthest away are chillier, so it might take a while to find a temperature which suits you.

Also, you can often close the blower vents, either fully or slightly, to make some areas warmer than others. We often do this when we have wet clothes / coats in the bathroom which we need to dry, but it's not cold enough to need heating elsewhere in the van.

Congratulations!

You're now in and the motorhome is set up. Crack open a bottle if you're done driving for the day. I hope you're feeling proud of yourself.

Of course, there are still things to do and systems to check, especially if this is your first night or if the van has been stood for a while.

Here's the order of what we'd do next:

- Let the dog out and go for a quick walk (remember to lock the van behind you.) Many campsites have dog runs to let them stretch their legs.
- If it's nice weather, get the awning out. If it's windy / raining- don't. Putting away the awning wet can cause it to mould.
- Get out your outdoor furniture- table, chairs and BBQ. Even better, start a campfire if allowed.
- Depending on time, either start dinner, or spending some time relaxing / reading some brochures from reception about nearby attractions.
- After food, make up the bed (unless you have a fixed or drop-down bed). We try not to leave this to the last minute (especially if we're enjoying some wine)- nothing worse than trying to make up the bed when tired or tipsy!

Some unwritten campsite rules

Most of these are common sense, so sorry if I'm stating the obvious, but just in case you don't know, here are some 'unwritten' rules for using campsites:

- Don't leave litter around- take it all to the bins onsite. Often there are recycling facilities, so use these if possible.
- Don't empty wastewater (or other waste!) on your pitch. This includes throwing washing up water into the bushes – unless the campsite has clearly stated you can do so – some sites like to use the water on their hedgerows so there is no water wastage but this maybe more common at smaller sites.
- Don't have loud music playing and obey any noise curfews in place.
- Pick up after your dog and dispose of it in the bins provided.
- Make sure your kids / animals aren't bothering anyone else nearby and make sure they are quiet by the curfew.
- Don't block access to anyone else's pitch or let your vehicle or awning hang out over onto the road.
- Don't run engines or motorhome generators if you can help it and definitely not in the evening or at night.
- Expect people to chat to you- especially if you have kids / animals. People are generally friendly and meeting new people is part of the fun of using campsites. Having said that, if someone's door is closed it usually means they don't want to chat.

Some more systems and things to check when you have time / inclination include:

- Check your hot water. Turn it on and make sure the water gets warm. Remember, it will take a while to warm up; much slower than you might be used to in your house.
- Test the lights inside the van- make sure they all work. Don't forget to check the outdoor light too- you'll use that a lot.
- Make up all the beds; check you have the right cushions etc.
- Set up the TV and / or internet and check it works and you can get a signal (see the 'life on the road' section).

Water usage

Don't forget that you don't have unlimited water in your van (unless you're on a serviced pitch. When you're showering or cleaning your teeth, you'll want to turn off the water until you're ready to rinse, instead of letting the water run.

Also, you'll have a MUCH smaller tank of hot water than you might be used to in a house. As a guide, we reckon we get around 5 minutes of hot water. Between the two of us.

The trick is to get wet, turn off water, lather, rinse, turn off water, repeat. It takes a little practise, but you'll get the hang of it.

For washing up, we tend to boil a little extra water in our gas kettle, and we use that instead of the hot water from the tank. We only turn the water heater on in the morning for a couple of hours, so once we've had a shower there's not a lot left until the next day!

You should be able to set the timer for the hot water on your control panel – as mentioned previously.

Unwind the awning

The motorhome awning confused the heck out of me the first time I did it. If you have an awning, you will probably have a winder (a long stick thing with a hook on one end.)

That hook goes into one end of the awning (there should be an eye) and then you start turning the base. *(Hopefully, that makes more sense when it's in front of you to see what I mean!)*

One way will tighten, the other will release. As the awning extends, it will get lower and lower. Eventually, you'll be able to reach it. The legs will generally be inside the front edge of the awning- pull them out and then twist them downwards to lower and extend to the desired height. You might want to use a couple of pegs to pin them down- use rock pegs on hard-standing pitches and put them in at an angle.

That probably sounds terribly confusing, but once you know, it all makes sense. Maybe try the awning out before you go- just so you know what to expect.

Also, don't get the awning out if strong winds or rain is forecast. They aren't very good in bad weather and if you put it away wet it will start to rot. Always leave the awning to dry out as much as possible before you put it away.

Our second motorhome with awning- in Giethoorn in Holland

Toilet talk

Ok, let's talk about the toilet. It always surprises me how many motorhome owners choose not to use their toilet onboard, but that's a personal decision for you to make. I guess if you're only planning on using a campsite with facilities, it's one less thing to worry about.

If you are going to use your toilet, you first need to check that the cassette is in place. Yes, it's possible to use the loo without anything being there to catch it- you don't want to get that wrong!

Next, you'll need to add appropriate toilet chemicals. The most common version are the blue and pink varieties, but we now use a green eco product which is fantastic and can be emptied in many more locations, especially in Europe where they use septic tanks more.

You basically need something which goes into the cassette and helps break down the waste. You can get liquid or tablets. Just put them into the toilet cassette (yep, straight down the hole where the 'business' goes) and you're good to go.

So to speak…

It usually works best with a bit of liquid, so we tend to add it when we first use the toilet after it's been emptied. You can add some water, but if you're trying to make you toilet last as long as possible between empties, this defeats the point.

You can buy a pink rinse. If you have a separate toilet flush tank, you can add some pink fluid to the tank. If your water comes from the main freshwater tank, you obviously can't add any pink, but you CAN buy a pink spray, which you spray onto the bowl before flushing and does the same job.

However, you don't NEED a pink rinse- it does nothing apart from making things smell nicer.

Also, you don't need to buy expensive toilet paper. We find that the more expensive the paper is, the less quickly it dissolves, which can make emptying the cassette a pain. You might want to abandon the Andrex in place of supermarket own brand.

Alternatively, you can put your toilet paper into a separate plastic or nappy bag and dispose of it in the trash. We've done this for years (life on a boat!) so it's normal for us.

An added benefit of this (apart from being able to use softer, thicker toilet paper), is that your toilet doesn't fill up so fast, so you can go longer between emptying. But if that's too weird, just do what works for you.

Leaving your pitch during your stay

If, during your stay, you want to leave the site or even the pitch in order to get water / empty waste, you'll need to disconnect everything (see below for full list.)

However, if you're just going for a day trip and coming back, be sure to leave an obvious sign that the pitch is reserved. Some people also leave their electric cable, so if you see a pitch with a cable on it, it's probably taken and you shouldn't use it.

Many campsites have barriers which they lock at night for safety, so be sure you're back before closing unless you have a fob. If you get back after dark, remember there could still be kids playing or people walking on the roads, so drive extra cautiously.

Also, parking up at night, using chocks and connecting everything can be a pain, so do try to get back before dark to make life easier until you're confident with what you're doing.

At the end of your stay

Sadly, the time will come when it's time to pack up and leave. You'll probably have a whole long list of things you want to buy / fix / improve- that's perfectly normal.

To pack up, just reverse the steps you took when you arrived. Start with winding up the awning, putting away all outdoor gear, then turning off gas, unplugging electric / water / waste, driving off chocks and making sure everything is put away safely. Go through the departure checklist again to be sure.

You will probably want to empty the toilet, water and waste tanks at the campsite- although you can empty the toilet at home if you prefer.

Empty the water waste – Grey Waste

Nearly every campsite has a grey wastewater disposal point. You can find out where this point is on your site map, then drive OVER it with your van until the drain is roughly below your waste disposal tap.

You will either have to physically open the outside drain valve on the van or you might be lucky and have an inside switch which opens the drain.

For an inside switch, you'll need to turn the engine off, turn the power on at the habitation control panel and open the waste tap.

Alternatively, you'll have a manual tap which you open under the motorhome to allow the tank to drain. Water will come gushing out (ideally into the drain!) and you just wait until it stops

Whichever you have, remember to close it again when the tank is empty!

TOP TIP: Try to wipe off as much food waste as possible when you wash up so it doesn't go down the drain into the tank. This will stop food waste and grease getting into the tank, which is hard to clean. This will also stop your tank smelling.

Emptying the toilet- Black / Chemical Waste

You'll probably want to wear gloves for this job.

Your toilet cassette is removable, usually through a flap door on the side of the motorhome. Take it out (if it's a Thetford, you probably have to push the orange handle in and up before you can pull it out.)

You'll also need to make sure the interior flap is closed on the toilet before you can remove the cassette.

Then, walk / roll it to the toilet / black waste disposal point- which is often a hole in the ground or a white disposal station (clearly marked- don't use just any hole in the ground!)

Unscrew the end of the cassette (ideally not over the hole in case you drop the lid!) and turn the cassette upside down over the hole. Yep, it will probably smell pretty bad.

Once empty, you'll usually see a hose at the station, which you can use to add some water to the cassette to rinse out. Do NOT use a freshwater hose for this job. I usually add a little water, then replace the lid, swill it all around again and empty; repeat until water comes out clear.

Make sure the cassette is totally empty before replacing it into the motorhome. Ours clicks shut- be sure it's in correctly!

Emptying the fresh water

You will probably have excess fresh water left in your tank. Don't leave this sitting there for weeks- it can go stagnant and nasty things can start growing in your tank.

If you're not going to be using the van for a while, empty the fresh water out at the same time and place as the grey waste- over the drain point. There will be two separate taps for this under your vehicle or you might have a fresh water dumping switch inside the van (usually near the grey waste. Don't get them confused!)

Please don't leave your taps open as you're driving, even if it is only fresh water; it's horrible for other roads users, particularly cyclists and gives us all a bad reputation.

Once the toilet, grey and freshwater have been emptied, you are ready to leave the site. Return any keys / fobs you had to the reception, or put them in the box by the exit, make sure the kids / dog / spouse are all safely onboard and you've removed any clothing you hung over the bike rack to dry.

Then you're free to drive to your next destination or return home. ☹

Things to do back home…

Once you're safely home, you'll want to do some final checks and a closedown. This should include:

- Closing all the blinds, vents and windows.
- We sometimes leave a small roof hatch open for ventilation- make sure rain can't get in! If in doubt, shut it all up and come back to air at least once every other week. We also pull across the fly net to stop bugs getting in.
- Remove all valuables, including the sat nav etc
- Empty and clean fridge.
- Remove all fresh / perishable food.
- Enable alarm and immobiliser and other motorhome security devices.
- Lock the cab and habitation doors.

And that's it! You've completed your very first trip in your new van. I hope it all went / will go smoothly- feel free to tag me on Instagram (@wanderingbird.adventures) and let me know where you ended up!

PART 6- LIFE ON THE ROAD

Great. We've covered the basics. You can plan a trip, get to a campsite and have a holiday in your van. Still, there are some more things to cover which aren't 'essentials', but can make life on the road a little easier, such as:

- TV
- Internet
- Laundry
- Towing
- Generators
- Security
- Accidents
- Travelling with pets
- Heading to Europe

So, let's dive into these!

TV

Installing or keeping a TV in your motorhome can be a controversial topic. Some people are vehemently against the idea, whilst others can't imagine being without it.

Personally, I'm of the opinion that your motorhome or camper is your domain, so use it however you like. Just be aware of the power drain with a TV, even for a 12v model and you'll need to find somewhere safe to store it if you don't fix it to a wall.

Also, remember to add the weight of a TV and any aerial / dish in your payload calculations.

Can You Use a Normal TV in a Motorhome?

There are a few key differences between a 'normal' household TV and one designed for motorhome or caravan use, including:

- Voltage
- Efficiency
- Robustness
- Ability to withstand vibrations.
- Weight

Most motorhome/ caravan TVs are powered by 12v and they are infinitely better at power management and more efficient than normal televisions.

Also, a motorhome TV is designed to be moved around, so it's more robust than a household TV, which is designed to stay in one place for most of its life.

A motorhome TV is designed to withstand the vibrations which come from being driven all over the place, not to mention the jolts and bumps from even the most careful driver.

Lastly, most household TVs weigh more than a motorhome TV. Sure, some of that is down to size, but it's also down to how they're designed, which helps keep you within your payload limits.

All this means that, unless you plan to watch a TV ONLY when you are plugged into mains in a campsite, you'll probably want a 12v TV, which will run off your motorhome leisure battery. Without the 12v capability, you can only use a 230v plug (like the one in your house that is also known as a 3-pin plug), which of course only works when you are plugged into the mains system.

I suppose you could also run it off a motorhome generator too, but you'd need a big generator with pure sine power, and it would be pretty heavy and noisy! But, again, it depends entirely on what sort of motorhoming holiday you want to have.

What is the Best TV for a Motorhome?

Aside from looking for a 12v motorhome TV, there are 2 main things to consider: Digital / Terrestrial or Satellite?

Terrestrial Digital Television (DVB-T)

DVB-T is the TV nearly everyone has in their home, at least in the UK. This is the method people use to get digital television, Freeview and most 'normal' television channels.

People get these channels at home by using an aerial and it's the same in a motorhome or caravan; you need an aerial (usually called a directional aerial).

This should be mounted as high up as possible, so is usually found on the roof, rear ladder or even an extendable pole.

A digital receiver has to be re-tuned at every new location, so whenever you stop and want to watch TV, you'll have to retune. This is done almost exactly the same way as at home; once the aerial is erected (if not permanently fixed in place), then you turn on the TV and start the tuning process. It takes a few minutes to complete.

Of course, it's entirely reliant on signal strength in the area; you'll find many campsite reviews mention whether or not a TV signal is good or not.

In order to use this system, you will need:

- A TV
- A DVB-T receiver or set-top box (capable of getting digital TV from an aerial – i.e., NOT a satellite receiver box).
- Television coaxial cable (25m seems to be the average length).
- DVB-T Aerial, either permanently fixed or magnetic.

NOTE: Many modern TVs now have DVB-T capability built-in, so you may NOT need a separate set-top box with these, but you will still need an aerial. If you want to install a permanent aerial, get one which is omni-directional and helps boost the signal.

You can also buy some set-top boxes and even a couple of 12v motorhome TVs with a built-in hard drive. This allows you to record one channel and watch another. They are often called PVRs (Personal Video Recorders) or DVRs (Digital Video Recorders).

Satellite Digital Television (DVB-S)

The second way to get TV in a motorhome or caravan is by satellite.

The biggest advantage of this method over terrestrial TV, is that it works in more areas; including those that may not have a digital signal. If you like to do a lot of wild / off-grid camping in your motorhome, satellite is possibly a better choice.

Also, if you plan to tour Europe, yet want to watch UK TV, you NEED satellite as digital will not work outside of the UK.

You can get many more channels on satellite; hundreds of television and radio stations which include BBC, ITV stations, SKY news (depending on package), Film 4 and many others. These are often called "Freesat" channels.

You can buy televisions with Freesat already built in, so you do not need to buy a separate box, but you will still need a satellite aerial (which will probably be some sort of mounted or freestanding dish) and a receiver.

If you'd like to know more about the best motorhome & campervan TVs on the market, you can check out our in-depth guide on the Wandering Bird website, which is regularly updated to review the latest and best models.

Watch Catch-up TV Online

Rather than carry a TV in our motorhome, we prefer to watch TV online. We realised that, in order to get UK TV in Europe, we either needed an expensive and heavy satellite system or needed to find a way to watch TV on the internet.

So, we use our laptops or iPads to access UK catch up apps (such as BBC iPlayer) from all over the world by using a VPN (virtual private network) which encrypts your online presence (and makes it look like you're in a different country to the one you're actually in.

It's not illegal to use one and we have used one for many years called Express VPN without any problems. We also subscribe to Amazon Prime and Netflix and watch both using Express VPN which has worked well for us.

Another option is to use a 'stick' which plugs into a laptop or a TV. Two of the most popular are:

- Amazon Firestick
- Roku stick

Again, you will need a Wi-Fi/ internet connection for either of these to work.

NOTE: We continue to pay for a UK TV licence. We still have one registered on the same address where our mail goes, which covers us for use when we are back in the UK and also when abroad. If you plan to watch TV in your motorhome, you'll still need a license.

Getting Internet on the Road

Obviously, in order to watch TV online, check Facebook, or visit websites you need to have internet access. You can either:

- Use the 4G / 5G data which is likely available on your phone/ iPad (you can use it as a hotspot for a laptop).
- Connect to a Wi-Fi network (like on a campsite).
- Connect to a portable dongle which creates its own network (as long as it has a signal) and you can then connect your devices to it over WI-FI.
- Install a specialist system / satellite internet on your motorhome.

Be aware, although many campsites offer Wi-Fi, they restrict it, so you will be unable to download movies or stream TV (stream means watch it in real-time). This can be frustrating (especially when there's a sporting match on) so if you have your own internet, you'll be much happier!

Using Your Phone or iPad for Mobile Wi-Fi or Internet Data

If you're in your home country, your mobile phone is most likely already set up to use data. As long as there is a phone signal, you should be able to connect to the internet on your phone (as long as your handset is less than about 10 years old).

You can also use your mobile phone as a Wi-Fi hotspot; meaning that other devices which DON'T have their own

SIM card (like a laptop or some iPads), can connect to your phone via a personal hotspot and use that data.

How to Set Up a Personal Hotspot for Your Phone

On an iPhone, for example, you can find your personal hotspot in the settings menu and follow the guidelines. Call it something easily recognisable and SET A PASSWORD, you don't want everyone else in the campsite logging onto your phone and using up all your data!

Open the device you want to use (e.g.- your laptop) and open the Wi-Fi settings. Find your phone's name in the Wi-Fi options. Select it, input the password and you'll be connected!

As long as you have a phone signal and mobile data, you're good to go. Remember, you'll be using data from your phone, so if you have a limit you'll need to pay after you've used that allowance, which can get very expensive, especially if touring overseas.

Using Mobile Data Outside Your Home Country

If you are travelling outside your home country, you'll need to use something called 'data roaming'. This means you can connect to a different network and still be able to use your data (3G/4G/5G). How much data you are able to use will depend on your monthly tariff.

Since BREXIT (for UK only), there are now spend caps and it's not as easy to use data roaming. If you plan to spend a lot of time in Europe, you might find it easier and cheaper to buy a European SIM card for a dongle or old phone and use that instead.

Don't forget, if you put a foreign SIM card into your phone, you won't be able to receive calls or texts on your normal number, so this why it's recommended to get an old device to use solely for internet.

Also, be aware that the data limit you have at home will probably NOT be the same as your allowance abroad. It's hard to track data usage, but things like maps, streaming videos and Facebook can all use up a LOT of data.

There are now spending caps, where UK networks are not allowed to charge you more than £45 / per month, per SIM card without asking your permission but once you hit that limit you'll not be able to access any data.

Some networks have gone back to charging a flat daily rate for using your data abroad, which can be expensive if you're overseas for several weeks. But check with your provider to be clear on what your contract allowance / limits are.

How to Use a Wi-Fi Dongle

The downside to using your phone for the internet is that it can use up all your mobile data very quickly if you're not careful, leaving you with a phone which is fairly useless.

For this reason, we use a Wi-Fi dongle for internet in our motorhome. We actually have 2 because we both work from the road, so we use a lot of data daily. We have one with EE and one with a European SIM.

As long as there is a phone signal, usually one of them is able to get decent internet access.

We often have 7 devices connected: two laptops, two iPads and 3 phones. And that's without our daughter being in the van!

Most people won't need that many devices, but if you're like us, it's important to check how many devices can be connected at once to the Wi-Fi dongle that you choose.

I should point out that we've never had a house with high-speed fibre broadband, so we're used to it. For many people, the slow speed of Wi-Fi internet can be a shock!

To use a dongle, you need to buy one (you can find ones we recommend on the Wandering Bird website), and you will also need to buy a SIM card to use in it.

Make sure you buy the correct size SIM card for the dongle. Many take nano-SIMs or micro-SIMs. If in doubt, go into a mobile shop and ask for advice once you have the dongle.

Prepaid SIMs are great but read the small print; often, once they're activated you only have so long to use the data before you lose it. We pay for our SIM monthly because we use it so often, but you need to do whatever works best for you.

Also, if you don't use the dongle for a long period of time (I think it's around 6 months) you might have to reactivate it before you can use it again, this should be mentioned in your instructions. Sometimes you even have to buy a new SIM card, but that's fairly easy to do; just swap them out, activate the new SIM and you're good to go again.

You'll need to connect your devices to the SIM once there's a signal. And don't forget, the dongle can't make a signal appear out of nowhere. If there's no network (like at the top of a mountain), it won't work.

Which Mobile Data Network Works Best?

Between us, we have devices on Three (3), Vodafone and EE. We often find huge differences in network coverage, both in the UK and in Europe. Many times, one network can't get a signal, while another one is full strength.

In our opinion, EE and Vodafone are great, and O2 apparently has good UK coverage too. You can do searches to see what network is best in your area or the area you want to go and choose accordingly.

How to Get Internet in the Middle of Nowhere

But what if there isn't a phone signal? What if you're in the middle of nowhere- can you get internet?

Some of our favourite nights in the motorhome have been when we haven't had internet- like the night we spent up the Swiss Alps under the Milky Way, planning how to change our lives.

Don't be scared of not having a phone/ Wi-Fi signal for the odd night- it's oddly liberating, even with teenagers.

The only way to get an internet signal if there are no other signals is by satellite. It can be done, but it is expensive and VERY slow. We used to use a satellite phone for internet when we were sailing... that was painful enough for us not to bother with it on the road!

Still, you can buy a satellite device for internet use - you'll need to speak to a specialist to get the best option for you.

Camped up by a lake in Austria, in the middle of nowhere

Motorhome Wi-Fi Internet Booster

A motorhome Wi-Fi booster is an antenna or small box which fixes to the roof of your motorhome / camper and boosts any Wi-Fi signal it receives, allowing you to get a better connection.

It can be fixed permanently or by suction caps, which might be better - as long as you remember to take it down before you drive off!!

We've used a booster on the boat for years, and they are very good. I really like the systems which can be powered by either 12v or 230v - perfect for mobile Wi-Fi when wild / off-grid camping or using on campsites. Again, for the best results, pop into a mobile specialist shop for specific advice on the latest models.

Motorhome roof antenna

A roof antenna amplifies and improves a Wi-Fi connection, such as from a campsite. It will NOT create a signal where there isn't one, but it can allow you to stream TV over a bad connection if needed.

You can fix an antenna or an aerial to the top of your motorhome to increase range. Just remember it will also increase your height, so be careful to take that into account for low bridges. Also, if you go above 3m in Europe, the cost of tolls will increase.

Doing Laundry on the Road

One thing which worries people new to motorhoming is how to do laundry whilst travelling. You'll be pleased to know that it's not as scary or confusing as it might seem.

There are several options available, which fall into the general categories of:

- Handwashing, normally in a sink or bucket.
- Carrying and using a laundry tub or bag (heck, some bigger motorhomes have a washer fitted in them!).
- Using a washer / dryer at a campsite.

- Visiting a laundrette / coin-operated laundromat in a nearby town.
- Using a Laundry service.

All of these are perfectly feasible, but there are some pros and cons to each.

Regardless of what method you use, you need to find somewhere to dry your clothes (if there is no tumble dryer facility available). In a motorhome you can pack a portable line dryer which are great and many fold down quite small.

You can also string up a line in the bathroom, especially if you have a heating vent in there.

Alternatively, just drape your clothes all over the van. You could even use an outside bike rack- although many campsites frown upon this. Having said that, they will tolerate wetsuits and swimming gear.

Also, be cautious if you leave your clothes outside overnight; many people have had things stolen (or pooped on by passing birds!

Laundry services are easy if you can find a good one, but they usually take a few days, so you'd need to be staying in the area for a while.

Also, be careful what you put in there - I've heard horror stories of people losing their nicer garments or getting the wrong things back.

Our favourite option is to use laundry facilities on a campsite. We usually make plans to stay on a campsite every 3 or 4 nights during a normal trip. It's normally quite easy to find a site which has a washing machine and dryer and choose to stay there.

You'll need to pay to use the washer (you'll either need to purchase tokens from reception or use coins).

If you can't find a campsite with a washer, you can always find and use a humble laundrette. It's been relatively easy to find one so far, and they're not too expensive (6-10€ per wash), quick (often done within 90 minutes) and we can usually plan it around our travelling.

To find one, type search terms into Google like 'coin-operated laundromat near me' or 'coin-operated laundromat in _____' (insert name of largish town.)

There are also more and more places where you can find washing machines outside supermarkets or petrol stations. This is fairly common across Europe and becoming more common in the UK. Search for 'Revolution'- they're the biggest brand and you'll find a map with locations on their website.

Towing / Second Vehicle

Most of the time, we tow 2 motorbikes on a trailer behind our motorhome. We've also done a couple of trips with a car behind us on a trailer- just for fun (my husband loves to restore old classic cars and bikes).

The reason we decided to buy a motorhome in the first place was because we wanted to explore Europe with our motorbikes. But we've also done several trips without the bikes (and trailer!) – so we know the pros and cons of motorhome towing and whether or not it's worth it

We love being able to bring our motorbikes with us and we've had some incredible adventures on the motorbikes. Some of our favourite biker roads include:

- Trollstigen road, Norway (you can drive this in a motorhome too- it's awesome).
- The Gorge road in the Italian Lakes (don't try this in a motorhome- it's through a cliff!).
- Black Forest, Germany - one of the best roads we've ridden anywhere.

Do you NEED a Second Vehicle?

One of the big discussions between buying a motorhome or a caravan, is what you do when you're on a campsite and want to go for a day trip. You either need to pack up your entire van so you can move it or leave it there and use public transport or a taxi, which can be a pain, especially if you want to go somewhere like the beach with all your gear. If you have a caravan, you can just use your car.

There have definitely been times where we've benefitted from having a second vehicle with us and it does make it a lot easier to pop to the shops or go exploring. But there are some serious downsides to towing, which is why the decision is never cut and dried.

For us, the main reason we tow the bikes is because we love riding. It's a fun hobby we do together and being able to visit incredible places and explore by bike is something which makes the downsides worthwhile. We have never chosen to take a modern car (like a smart car) because we don't see the need, but we have toured with a classic car a couple of times which was fun.

Still, it's usually possible to get everywhere you need to go by other means.

Many people choose to carry bicycles or electric bikes, which are a great idea. Just remember that the weight goes into your payload *(sick of me saying that yet?!)*

Some other people travel with both the motorhome and someone driving a car. I can certainly see the advantages of this, but you also have the disadvantages of double the fuel costs and not travelling together (although that might also be an advantage!)

Again, there are no strict rules, if that's what works for you, then do that!

Downsides of Towing

There are quite a few downsides of towing, which is why not many people do it. The main ones are:

- It can be harder to park.
- Some campsites or Aires don't allow trailers.
- It can make the cost of travelling more expensive (ferries/ tolls are more, plus extra costs in campsites).
- Going up and down mountains can be a pain, especially if the roads are narrow.
- It can affect the speed you are allowed to drive at (for example- max. 60mph on a UK motorway.)
- You are also not allowed to use the outside lane on a motorway.

I've expanded on some of those below.

Does towing make it harder to drive the motorhome?

Towing ANYTHING makes driving harder, or at least more complex. However, towing a trailer or a small car behind a motorhome normally isn't as difficult as towing behind a car, because the motorhome is so much bigger.

But yes, parking, reversing or manoeuvring in tight spaces is harder with a trailer or car attached. You also need to be more careful with your route - not on motorways or main roads, but in small villages where turning might be tough. Or in petrol stations, which can be surprisingly hard to get out of!

Does having a trailer or car cost more on ferries/ tunnel?

Oh yes. This is one of the biggest downsides for towing in our opinion, the sheer cost of it.

Now to be clear, towing doesn't actually cost much more in terms of our mpg. So, if you live and travel in the UK only, you won't have many additional costs for taking a trailer - except for some campsite fees.

But...

If you are planning a trip to Europe, you really need to weigh up the pros and cons of taking a trailer or car with you. Because EVERYTHING costs more.

- The ferry / tunnel is priced based on your length.
- Tolls in many countries cost more, as you become a CAT 3 (3 axles), instead of a CAT 2).
- If you travel to Norway ALL the small ferries are also priced on length, so they cost more.
- Campsites often charge extra for a trailer or car
- Aires in Europe sometimes charge for longer vehicles.

- Car parks which require a parking ticket may require 2 or even 3 as you take up additional spaces. ⎯

In short, it can definitely be more expensive.

Does towing affect where you stay?

Yep. When we're towing, we have much less flexibility over where to stay. We don't tend to use campsites in Europe very often as we prefer Aires or wild / off-grid camping.

But many Aires are only suitable for campers up to 7m long. (Which is one of the biggest reasons we downsized our motorhome!)

We've never had a problem finding somewhere to stay, eventually, but we have definitely had to drive past some pretty park ups because we couldn't fit, and it's taken us longer or we've had to stay further away from somewhere than we might have liked.

Also, not all campsites accept trailers, so we need to be careful if we do choose to stay on a site. It's not insurmountable (after all, we still continue to tow, so it can't be that bad) but it's definitely not as 'easy' as life without a trailer.

Motorhome insurance with a trailer

Obviously, if you're taking more, you're going to need to insure more - which increases the costs.

Make sure it is VERY clear who insures what. We once found ourselves in a situation where our motorhome insurer, insured the van and trailer while towing, and our bike insurer insured the bikes while riding, but NO-ONE insured the bikes whilst they were ON the trailer being towed. (Took us ages to get it straightened out!)

You also need to make sure your insurance covers you and the motorhome while towing - not all do, even if you are legally allowed to tow.

Is it legal to tow with a motorhome or campervan?

Yes, as long as you & the vehicle are within the motorhome towing laws, it's absolutely fine to tow with a motorhome.

Here's what you need to know:

- Firstly, you need to check if you are allowed to tow on your licence.
- Then, you need to check how MUCH weight you can tow on your licence.
- Lastly, you need to check if your insurance covers you for towing.

What is the motorhome allowed to tow?

Ok, bear with me. I'm about to spew acronyms at you. You need to know a couple of numbers.

First, you need to know what the weight of your motorhome / camper is when fully loaded. This includes all passengers, pets, fuel, water, gas, food, clothes, paddleboards - EVERYTHING.

Go to a weighbridge when the van is packed and get an exact weight. *Hopefully you'll be under the MTPLM!*

NOTE: MTPLM and MAM (maximum authorised Mass) are the same thing- the max weight the vehicle/ trailer can be loaded to. MAM usually is used to refer to caravans or trailers.

Next, you need to know the weight of the car or trailer you want to tow behind the motorhome. This is the weight of the trailer and the vehicle(s), so for example, the weight of the trailer with our 2 motorbikes on it.

Your Gross Train Weight (GTW) restriction is the weight of the motorhome (fully laden) and the trailer / car (fully laden) TOGETHER.

So, if your motorhome weighs 3 tonnes fully laden, and your trailer weighs 750kg, your GTW would be 3.75 tonnes.

THEN, you need to make sure you are under the GTW that your motorhome is ALLOWED to pull. This is often on a plate inside the driver or passenger door, but if not, this information should be on your paperwork or online in the specs for your model van.

If you have a UK driving licence, be aware the law for towing changed recently changed. Now, everyone is allowed to tow a trailer up to 3,500kg MAM, as long as the combined weight of vehicle and trailer doesn't exceed the vehicles max GTW.

Don't panic if you need to read that section several times. It took me a while to understand it all too!

The towbar and its towing capacity

Another thing to consider is the tow bar weight capacity.

There are some trailers / backboxes which sit on the nose of the tow bar. You need to make sure the towbar nose can take the weight you want to put on it. You find this out from your towbar fitter.

The same applies with towing weight - check this with your towbar fitter and make sure it is enough to accommodate what you want to tow.

If you are planning to put a lot of weight directly onto the towbar, then you need to consider your motorhome loading and if the rear axle of the van can take the weight and how it will affect steering etc (most motorhomes have front-wheel drive).

Don't expect just ANY towbar fitting company to be able to fit a towbar to a motorhome. We tried several and had to drive nearly 100 miles to find someone who could do it - it's a fairly specialist job.

So, is it worth it?

After all that, you probably think we're mad for towing. But it comes down to personal choice and why you're travelling in the first place.

If you prefer campsites near big attractions with easy access to trains, buses or even hire cars, then you probably don't need to tow anything.

If you head off into the wilds and want to be as discreet as possible and / or keep costs down, you probably don't want to or won't need to tow.

But, if you like to stay on a campsite and not move for a while then you might want another vehicle to pop to shops or local attractions. Towing a car with you makes sense in that situation - or perhaps hire one in the local area for a few days.

For us, we just love being able to ride our bikes in beautiful areas during the summer. It's worth it for us which is why we continue to take them on most of our trips.

Generator/ Power Banks

I said all the way back up in Part 2 that most people do NOT need a generator in their motorhome or campervan. Seriously, save the payload and your money for something else; like an awning or solar panels.

BUT, for anyone who loves spending time off-grid, away from services and campsites, and wants to do that the majority of the time, a generator can be really useful.

Also, if you enjoy festivals, rallies or events, you often have to stay in a field with no hook-up, but which allows generators. It really is all down to how you choose to use your van.

We decided to get a generator when we were heading up to Norway, where they allow wild / off-grid camping almost anywhere.

And I'm glad we did, because it allowed us to stay for an extra night or two in some INCREDIBLE locations, without worrying about how to charge the laptops when we needed to work. For us, it was invaluable but only because we work from the road.

Now though, there are proper power banks (which weren't so affordable when we started touring.) These are basically a portable battery which you can use to power devices like laptops or charge batteries whenever you like.

I find them MUCH easier to use than a generator and they're easier to store too. No need to carry cans of fuel or service them - they just need recharging when you're driving. For this reason, we no longer carry a generator- we have a power bank.

Downsides of a Motorhome Generator

There are several downsides to carrying a generator onboard your motorhome or camper:

- Initial cost
- Space- finding somewhere to store it.
- Weight- it eats into your motorhome payload.
- Having to carry fuel for it.
- Maintenance
- Noise

- How to choose the right motorhome generator for you.

Let's be honest, most of us are conditioned to think that bigger is better (no sniggering in the back row please… ☺)

However, you don't need to buy the biggest portable generator possible, even if you can fit it into a locker and you magically have the payload to spare.

There are several things to look for:

- Physical size.
- Weight (both to lift AND towards your motorhome payload).
- Power output level (and frequency) – UK is 230v/ 50hz.
- Noise output level
- Fuel type
- Socket type
- Starting method (I HATE pull starts, even though that's what we have- but button starts are so much easier!

What size generator do you need?

There are two types of size to consider - the physical size of the generator, and the amount of power it produces.

Don't forget, we're talking about portable generators, not permanently fitted generators like you get in American RVs or boats. Portable generators are only designed to be run for a few hours at a time, not permanently.

Physical size

Physical size is fairly obvious; does it fit where you want it to go when it's being stored? If you need to put it under a seat inside the van (as we do), or you're lucky enough to have a motorhome with a garage or external storage locker, you need to make sure it will physically fit where you want.

Don't forget to consider height, as well as width and depth - many potential motorhome generators are too tall to go under a seat, especially those with a cross beam.

We also don't have a generator with wheels, as it takes up too much room. However, if you have a garage, you might prefer a type with wheels so it's easier to move, especially if you have a ramp.

Weight

Another consideration is weight. Obviously for payload, but also because you'll need to lift it in and out of your motorhome or camper. If it's too heavy, you're either going to injure yourself or never use it because it's impossible to get out, which defeats the point of buying it.

As a (very) rough guide, a 1000w model weighs about 15kg, but a 2000w generator could weigh over 20kg.

How much power do you need?

So, what power output do you need? What amount is sufficient?

The obvious answer is 'the amount which allows you to run and use whatever you want to run and use'. If you just want to top up your leisure battery, or you're your phones/ iPads a quick charge, you can get away with as little as a 1kw generator.

If you want to use any appliance which is over 1000w in power (look at the label on the device), then you'll need a generator capable of handling that. For example, many standard hair dryers are 1800w. To run one, you'd need a generator of at least 1800w PLUS a bit more (around 20%) for resistance and other loads.

If you're planning to use your generator for something with moving parts (like a pressure washer), you need to add even more for resistance; around 30-50% on top of the power requirement.

NOTE: Many portable generators have a 'maximum' wattage and a 'constant/continuous wattage' value. This means it can handle a higher load for a short period of time (whilst starting up an air conditioning unit or heater for example), but then it needs to drop down to a running level.

Look at the constant/ continuous or running wattage as the main figure for prolonged use.

If you'd like to know the current best models of motorhome generators, pop onto www.wandering-bird.com and search 'generators', so you can choose which one is the best for you in terms of power, noise levels and other factors.

Motorhome Security

It's important to be aware of security with a motorhome or camper. No one likes to consider what 'could' happen but being prepared is more sensible than pretending it's not a possibility.

There are several types of motorhome security we're concerned with:

- Security of your van at night while you're sleeping inside.
- Security of your van when you leave it for a few hours to explore while travelling.
- Security of your van whilst NOT travelling- either at home or in storage.

Let's break down each one below.

Motorhome Safety While Travelling

It's hard to say whether vans are more vulnerable at home or while out and about on the road. Certainly, most vehicle thefts seem to happen at home, whilst most possession-based thefts happen while travelling.

To start, let's look at ways to improve safety while out on the road,

We've been touring Europe in our motorhome for several years and have never been the victim of theft (touch wood!) I know that might just be dumb luck, but we do our best to assess the odds and act accordingly.

We also listen to our gut and try to remove ourselves from situations we're not happy with, such as leaving our vehicle unattended in a place we don't like the feel.

Security at Night

Staying safe at night in a motorhome or campervan while you're travelling can feel like a challenge. If you're not used to it, it can feel isolating and vulnerable to spend the night in a plastic / tin box instead of bricks and mortar. Also, everything seems scarier at night - noises and passing cars can make you jumpy.

Let's look at this logically. When you stay in a motorhome overnight, you're generally going to be on one of 3 places:

- A proper campsite (usually with a barrier or gate).
- Aire / approved motorhome parking spot.
- Wild camping / Off-grid.

We'll look at physical devices and tricks / tips a little later, but let's assess the 'odds' at each of the above 3 locations.

Campsites: Most campsites we've stayed at have had some form of barrier, preventing people from just driving in. This makes it very difficult (although not impossible) for people to drive onto a site and steal your van, as they normally need some form of code or key to exit.

Of course, there are exceptions, but very few vehicle thefts happen from proper campsites. That doesn't mean you don't get petty theft on sites, such as stolen outdoor furniture or clothes, but actual vehicle theft is low if there's adequate protection.

Aires / Approved Spots: Whether you're using an Aire in Europe, staying on a Brit stops car park or CL site in the UK, the risks are roughly the same.

These locations are approved for motorhome stopovers, but usually have no barriers or cameras for night-time security.

The biggest risks here are opportunists. Since you're staying somewhere which is a known place for motorhomes to stop at, local thieves can potentially swing by whenever they want, to see who's arrived.

In my opinion, some places are riskier than others. We avoid sleeping / stopping at:

- Motorway services or Aires on the motorways in Europe, even if they do offer free overnight parking.
- Avoid places near big cities. Again, you're more likely to get opportunists or thieves in areas with more people- that's just simple maths.

I'm not saying we don't go to cities, just that we'll use a proper campsite instead of an Aire wherever possible, even if it costs a little more.

We also rarely leave our van unattended at a Brit Stops or car park. If we want to ride our motorbikes, we'll book into a campsite.

If we're in a nice Aire, with a barrier and lots of other vans around, we might leave it while we go exploring for a couple of hours, but usually we prefer a campsite with better security.

Wild / Off-grid Camping: I remember how terrifying wild / off-grid camping felt when we started doing it. Partly, I was worried about being arrested, but mostly I was worried about being murdered in my sleep. Or robbed.

But here's what you need to remember: When you are wild / off-grid camping- NO ONE KNOWS WHERE YOU ARE.

As long as you haven't posted it on Facebook - please don't do that until you are leaving or have left!

Although some spots will be known as potential motorhome stopovers, you'll mainly be dealing with passing opportunists, which means your task is to make your van look like a difficult target to steal, with security devices, surveillance (fake or real) or increased protection like additional locks (see below).

We also listen to our gut feelings. Obviously, we don't pick a wild / off-grid camping spot thinking it's going to be dodgy, but when we arrive, we generally get a 'feeling'.

In the past, we have ignored these feelings twice - and both times we've regretted it. Nothing happened to our van, but we spent the night on edge and not sleeping well, due to being alert to noises or any problem which might occur. Not the best way to spend an evening and being on edge isn't fun!

Don't forget, you are not a tree. The beauty of being in a home on wheels is that you can move, even in the middle of the night.

There have been a couple of occasions where we've found ourselves in a car park which has become unexpectedly "sociable" in the middle of the night. Considering we had our daughter with us, we decided to just drive off. Quickly.

Security Devices

There are plenty of devices and security gear you can buy to protect your vehicle, both at home and on the road.

These include:

- Wheel clamps for motorhomes or caravans.
- Steering locks for motorhomes.
- Making the vehicle undriveable.
- Motorhome or camper alarm.
- Motorhome or camper security camera.
- Trackers & Immobilisers
- Improve Motorhome security door locks.

If you would like to know our latest recommendations, just search 'security' on the wandering-bird.com website.

Extra Door Security

You can fit additional cab and habitation (hab) door locks, although please do measure your doors carefully as not all locks will fit all van types.

Additionally, you can carry a locking cab bar, which effectively locks the two cab doors together so they can't be opened.

Extra Window Security

Motorhome windows are a known weak point. By far the BEST type of window to have on your van is a sliding one but most motorhomes don't have those.

You can get lots of window sensors, but very few will stop a window being forced open.

One of the best options, although it's not suitable for every van or motorhome, is to get a child window restrictor, so the window only opens so far.

Motorhome Security - Tips to Protect Your Possessions While Travelling

Campsites

The sad fact is that most thefts on campsites occur from other people sharing the site with you. These are people looking for 'lucky' opportunities, such as clothes or kit left out overnight or while the van is unattended.

The easiest way to prevent this is not to leave anything out, including kayaks, wetsuits, towels etc.

We try to combat theft by putting our wet kayak & paddleboard on the motorhome roof overnight-which works great as long as it's not windy!!

Aires

This is a tough one, as most thieves know that you will be leaving your vehicle to visit the local town or attraction at some point; after all, that's why you're there. And, sadly, they do keep watch.

There is no easy solution against this. We use a range of methods to try and stop our possessions being stolen or the van being vandalised whilst we're not with it- we'll get to those shortly.

All you can do is ensure your vehicle looks as difficult to get into as possible.

Those extra locks mentioned above, and some well-placed stickers are more than most people have, which makes your van look not worth the effort.

We've met people with 'German Shepherd on board' stickers, when they don't have a dog at all, let alone a German Shepherd!

We have stickers warning people that the motorhome is always under camera surveillance (it is, as we have wireless surveillance onboard, but you can always buy them even if you don't have a camera.)

Wild / Off-grid Camping

We rarely leave our van unattended for longer than about half an hour while wild / off-grid camping and never at night. We might go for a short walk, but if we want to ride our motorbikes or visit a local attraction, we will take the motorhome to a campsite where it will be safer.

The only exception to this was while we were touring Norway. That is the safest country we have ever visited, and we merrily left our van at the side of a road and went off on the motorbikes all day without concern. I wish everywhere was like that!

Other tips to secure your motorhome while travelling

Don't ever hand over your keys!

No campsite should ever ask for your keys (although some may ask for your passport).

Close doors, windows & vents before you leave

Make sure you lock up properly before leaving. The obvious exception to this is if you are leaving a dog behind in the motorhome, you MUST leave them some air.

If you are travelling in a hot country, please remember how quickly a vehicle can heat up in the sunshine and don't leave your dog alone. But otherwise, shut everything up tight.

Remove things from sight

If you have a tv or a sat-nav, remove it from view and hide it somewhere safe. Same advice for iPads, laptops, phones and other electrical devices.

Some people recommend leaving something 'easy' on display so the thieves feel like they've 'got something', but honestly that just feels like you're encouraging people to break in. We lock everything down.

Find a secret hiding place

You might be able to find a spot in your van which works well for valuables. We don't recommend bringing jewellery with you at all if you can avoid it and always take your passport, phone and wallet with you when you leave the van. But you might find a locker, or a hidden spot, which allows you to hide a laptop or iPad.

If you have an electric drop-down bed which locks, our favourite place in our last van was on top of that bed and then remove the key. Without the key, it was almost impossible to get the bed down (just don't lose the key!!)

Sadly, all you can do is your best. Some thieves are very good at their job. As with a house, make sure your insurance covers you, do your best to prevent break-ins and opportunistic theft, and then don't spend hours obsessing over it or you'll drive yourself crazy.

Dealing with Accidents

No matter how much you prepare and/or plan for your road trip, accidents do happen. If you're British and live in the UK, you probably already know how to deal with an accident:

- get the other persons details, including their name, address and insurer details
- take plenty of photos
- as long as no-one is injured and the Police or other services aren't required or involved, then you can continue your journey if you are able.

IMPORTANT: Leaving the scene of an accident without providing your information is considered an offence and you will be prosecuted. Stay at the scene until you are told you can go by the Police or until the other parties leave.

TIP: Make sure you have the details of your breakdown cover and your insurer somewhere easily accessible. Many people pop it on a piece of paper inside the sun visor, so it's easy to find should you need to.

Travelling with Pets

One of the best things about motorhome travel is that we can take our dog with us. Mac is a Cocker Spaniel, and he LOVES van-life. Seriously, he gets so excited about turning up and discovering a new place.

I'm sure if you have a dog or pet and are planning to go to Europe from the UK, you've heard all about the new laws concerning pet travel. If not, we'll share the current rules shortly.

But first, let's cover some basic tips for travelling and living with a pet in a motorhome or camper van.

The most important thing is to make sure they are safely secured whilst you're travelling. Nobody ever plans to brake suddenly, but if it happens you could injure both them and you if they get flung forwards.

Make sure they have a proper holding point and secure them in a harness, not to their collar.

We used to travel with Mac in a small fabric crate, until he realised he could literally claw his way out of it. We worried about putting him in a metal crate, so now he wears a lightweight harness with a lead which clips to a seat.

He prefers sitting up on the seat, it always makes me laugh to look back and see him looking out the window.

If we're travelling with both our daughter and Mac, they fight for the window seat (Mac usually wins!)

Despite his best attempts, Mac doesn't ride in the front seats; he is secured in the rear ones.

You might also want to set up a specific area for their bed. We had such good intentions with Mac when he was a puppy… but I'm sorry to say he now sleeps on the bed with us and chills wherever he feels like it in the van. But if you have a pet bed, make sure they know where it is.

Also, remember how hot vehicles can get in summer. A motorhome is just a bigger version of a car, and I wouldn't want to be locked inside one on a hot sunny day with no air.

We rarely leave Mac unattended in the van, but if we do, it's for no longer than an hour and never when it's warm.

There have been loads of museums or attractions we've not been able to visit, but that's the price of travelling with our favourite furry buddy. *(Having said that, right now he's chewing a sock, trying to get my attention. Perhaps 'favourite' is a little strong…!!)*

Travelling in Hot Weather

Heatstroke is a very real problem, especially in athletic dogs like ours who just run… and run... and run. I once took Mac for a walk about 9am one morning and hadn't fully appreciated how hot he was getting.

After about 20 minutes of him running around, he lay down in the ditch, panting hard and refused to move.

After a few minutes of watching him, I had to climb in (yep, into the nettles!), pick him up and carry him back to the van.

He's only 15kg but he was like a dead weight; thank goodness we didn't get a Labrador!

He was suffering from over-heating (even at 9am!) and it took ages to cool him down again.

Some tips for keeping dogs cool during hot, sunny days:

- Go for a walk early, before it heats up. I've been known to get up at 6am to walk Mac (and even then, it's warm enough for shorts and t-shirt!)
- Take water for them to drink with you, even on short walks.
- Refuse to play ball if it's too hot, even when your over-excited pup really REALLY wants to play.
- Don't let them out in the hottest part of the day (12-3pm). Keep them in the shade where possible. It can be hard to plan your sightseeing

around this, but you'll probably be glad of a rest and a siesta then too.

- Make sure they have plenty of access to clean, cool drinking water.
- Invest in a cool jacket or mat. Mac hates the mat, but he loves his cool jacket, which we wet down and keep in the fridge. We have two, so he can be wearing one while another is chilling.

How to Tell If a Dog is Overheating

Heatstroke is serious in dogs, so learn these signs:

- Is there excessive panting/ drooling.
- Are they collapsed or vomiting?
- Are they lethargic, confused, or uncoordinated?
- Excessive drowsiness. This is a tough one as on hot days our dog (and us!) sleep way more than usual. But keep an eye on them if they're sleeping a lot.

How to cool down a dog which is overheating

Cooling down an overheated dog is not easy. Dogs don't sweat in the same way we do, and when they get hot it's not easy for them to regulate their body temperature.

If you suspect your dog is overheating, or need to cool down an excessively panting dog, take them to shade and cool them down gradually.

Put them in water if possible (not deep water) or put cool, damp towels/ cool jacket on them. A cool towel on their belly can help too. Give them tepid water to drink, but only small amounts at a time. A cool (not cold!) shower is also a good idea if you can.

Things to feed a hot dog

NOTE: These food tips are for 'normal' hot dogs, NOT overheating dogs. Don't give an overheating dog ice cubes or anything frozen- they could go into shock. Cool them down gradually.

You can feed them cold meat. Normally, Mac eats kibble with tinned wet food as a treat, but I've been freezing chunks of meat to keep him cool.

Frozen berries like raspberries, strawberries and blueberries are an awesome treat for dogs. The antioxidants are good for their joints, and they'll love the cool treat. Just keep it to a small handful a day and NOT every day. Be careful of wild berries from hedgerows, some wild berries are toxic to dogs.

Another great treat is dog friendly peanut butter smeared onto a chew toy and frozen, Mac LOVES it.

You can give them ice cubes but not if you suspect they have heatstroke; it can be too much of a shock for them.

Can dogs eat ice cream?

Short answer? Yes, but not a lot and not often. Adult dogs can't tolerate lactose and the sugar isn't good for your dog. Be careful of the flavour of ice cream chocolate, macadamia nuts and raisins are all toxic to dogs. We only let Mac have vanilla or fruit flavour and then it's literally less than a spoonful.

Still, he loves licking our empty ice cream cartons… and then ripping them to shreds!

There are also specific dog ice-cream treats you can get but may not always be available where you are.

I'm sure there must be similar advice if you travel with cats or other pets but please do check with your vet before you travel.

Processionary Pine Caterpillars

If you're a pet owner, you've probably heard about these 'woolly' caterpillars but, just in case, here's what you need to know. They are a type of caterpillar in Europe (and now in the UK) which is poisonous to dogs (and cats, I think). They are 'furry' and have thousands of fine hairs on their bodies.

If a dog sniffs them, the hairs (which are covered in a toxin) affect the dog almost like an allergic reaction, causing tongue, throat and stomach to swell until they can't breathe.

If your dog starts salivating whilst scratching his mouth, get them to a vet quickly. Really quickly.

These caterpillars grow on pine trees and come down to the ground when the weather gets warmer (usually end February - May.)

They're looking for a place to bury themselves before they re-emerge as moths. Being poisonous is the only thing which stops them being vulnerable to predators.

So, if you are camped or parked up near pine trees, be very vigilant. They generally walk in a long line, hence processionary and are fairly easy to spot and avoid.

You can read more about about touring with pets in our Vanlife with Dogs book.

Heading to Europe

It's natural that, once you get the hang of this motorhoming lark, you'll start setting your sights on places further and further away. For many people, that includes travelling to Europe.

We've already provided lots of tips to get you ready in this book, but if you'd like specific advice for motorhoming in Europe, which includes further details on using Aires, campsites, finding free places, getting gas, water and loads more helpful tips, you might enjoy our Europe Toolkit.

Check it out at **wandering-bird.com/ motorhome-guide-ebooks/**

Motorhoming in the Italian Dolomites- the entire area is breath-taking

PART 7- CARING FOR YOUR VEHICLE

I have GOOD NEWS!! The huge majority of what you need to do for regular motorhome or camper maintenance has already been covered in the pre-trip checks, back in Part 4.

Motorhome Maintenance

Motorhome maintenance is something which intimidates a lot of new owners, but there's no real need, if you're unsure, there are plenty of professionals who can help, even if it's just for the first year when your experience may be limited.

The main times for maintenance are:

- De-winterising / checks before the first big trip of the year (pre-trip checks).
- After a period of not being used (pre-trip checks).
- Annual maintenance (can be combined with a hab (habitation) check if you so choose).
- If you discover a problem.

There are two main types of maintenance:

- Vehicle / Engine
- Habitation

We'll cover both below.

I've also gone into more detail with looking after your leisure battery and cleaning in this section, as doing both of those correctly will extend the life of your vehicle & battery considerably.

Servicing the Engine

Engine / mechanical servicing involves looking after the chassis and engine of your motorhome and should be carried out at certain regular intervals, usually every two years (or at 30k mileage intervals if sooner). Your manual will have a suggested service guide.

It's recommended to have an oil and filter change more frequently, due to the relatively low number of miles covered over a 2-year period, and because diesel engines don't like 'sitting around'.

You also need an annual MOT (if you have a UK registered vehicle) or whatever the equivalent is in your country.

This however does not apply to new vehicles as the first MOT due on a new vehicle is 3 years from registration date but you can use the Gov.uk website and enter your number plate / registration number.

This ensures that the vehicle is safe and road worthy. Many people choose to get an engine service done at the same time as an MOT.

If you get your engine serviced, make sure they cover:

- Changing the engine oil and filters.
- Checking all lines, pipes and hoses.

- Checking all rubber components which can corrode or split.
- Check, change and adjusting belts where necessary.
- Check and cleaning the air filter.
- Check and top up fluid levels.
- Check washer fluid and wipers.
- Check and adjust handbrake.
- Check tyre wear and pressure.
- Check brakes front and back, including pads and discs.
- Check all vehicle lights.
- Check and re-gas air con if needed.

Engine servicing prices vary hugely depending on vehicle and location, but you can expect to pay upwards of £150 for the check, plus any parts & labour or extra work needed.

Hab Checks / Regular Maintenance

It's a good idea to also regularly check and service the living area of your motorhome. This is called a habitation check (hab check).

A habitation check is NOT a mandatory requirement unless it's required for your insurance or if you need to maintain a warranty.

It's perfectly ok to drive and use a motorhome which hasn't had a hab check for years, as long as you have in-date insurance, MOT and tax.

Having said that, you've invested a lot of money into your motorhome or camper. Regular habitation checks not only keep you and your family safe, but it will help with keeping the value of the vehicle when you come to sell it.

If you come to sell your vehicle privately in the future, you will probably be expected to provide a recent habitation check as part of the agreement, so the buyer can see if there are any potential problems.

You can do your own 'hab check' each year if you feel comfortable doing so, but to sell the vehicle they'll expect one done by a professional.

Things we strongly suggest (even if your insurance doesn't) that you check or get checked each year include:

- Electrical system (including Fridge)
- Gas system
- Any safety appliances or gear, including spare tyre.
- Water and waste system
- Checking the bodywork/ interior for leaks/ signs of damp or damage.

You can request a habitation check from an appropriate garage at any time. Most people choose to do them at the start of the year or after a period of long storage.

If you'd like to do the same, book as far in advance as possible, they get booked up months in advance. Again, you are free to use your vehicle without a habitation check as long as you are insured.

You can get a hab check done in many places. Many motorhome dealers offer the service (for a fee), as do some bigger garages.

It works a bit like an MOT- you drop the van off with them and they'll do a thorough inspection, highlighting any issues to you. This is usually done the same day as you drop it off.

If you have a vehicle with a wooden frame (instead of the more modern ones), then you might wish to get a check done more frequently (perhaps twice a year), just in case there is any damp discovered; rot can be lethal to a wooden frame, so the quicker you discover it, the quicker you can fix it.

Again, the price of a hab check can vary greatly. Our last one cost us around £290, which included a gas safety check. All in all, it took about 4 hours.

Approved Workshops

There are places which are 'Approved Workshops', a group of independently assessed workshops, regulated by the NCC (National Caravan Council), The Caravan and Motorhome Club and The Camping and Caravanning Club.

There are currently over 500 fixed and mobile Approved Workshops across the UK. In order to be accepted in the Scheme, workshops must pass an annual inspection by a team of independent assessors and must comply with the Scheme's standards.

What to Expect from a Hab Check

Here's what to expect during your hab check:

The engineer will need access to everything in the van, so have keys available for all lockers and the garage etc.

Clear out as much personal gear as possible. They need to get everywhere to check for damp or areas of ingress, especially in garages or lockers, and not having to move things around will make it easier to spot problem areas.

They will usually drain your water system, so don't bother filling it before the check.

They will need gas in the bottles to do a gas check (some places can provide their own bottles if you don't have one but check in advance).

If they are coming to you, they will need a mains electric connection going into the van so they can check the sockets and other electrical systems. They'll also need to see and check your leisure battery.

Example Habitation report (available free from the Approved Workshops website)

Cleaning Your Van

Let's be real, most of us know how to clean. We are perfectly capable of cleaning our houses, cars, clothes etc but cleaning a motorhome, campervan or caravan for the first time can be daunting.

You DON'T want to:

- Use any cleaning product which might cause damage or an adverse reaction.
- Pressure wash the wrong thing and cause a leak or damage.
- Use the wrong cleaning brush and scratch that expensive hunk of plastic.

The other frustrating part is when you spend HOURS cleaning your motorhome, and then two days later the dreaded black streaks are back!

The good news is, once you've found a cleaning system and products which work for you, you're set for a while *(until the next motorhome show at least, when you'll discover a NEW miracle motorhome cleaner...!)*

Here's a List of Things We Recommend for Cleaning Your Motorhome or Campervan:

- Somewhere to clean it.
- Water- either a hose, bucket or pressure washer (we'll talk more about the dangers of pressure washing later).
- Ladder or way of reaching your motorhome roof.
- Extendable or long-handled brush.

- Washing mitt (sponges are fine if used once, but can retain grit which could scratch your van).
- Motorhome cleaner
- **Window cleaner** for both glass and acrylic windows (assuming you have them).
- Wheel and tyre cleaner.
- **Finishing product for protection and shine.**
- Microfibre drying cloth (better than a chamois leather- and cheaper!)
- Toothbrush for cleaning seals.
- Headphones and your favourite podcast or music…. you're going to be here a while.

If you'd like to see the products we currently use and love to clean our motorhome, head to **wandering-bird.com/mms**

When cleaning, start with the roof. That way, all the streaks and trickles from the roof won't ruin all your hard work of washing the body. Also, try to pick an overcast but not windy or rainy day, so your van won't dry with streaks.

If you can't do this, completely wash, rinse and finish one side before starting another. Lastly, rinse out cloths in clean water regularly to remove dirt.

Where to Clean Your Motorhome

One thing to consider is access to water. If you're cleaning your motorhome or camper at home, then you're likely to have a good supply of water.

However, if your motorhome is in storage, it's very likely that you won't have access to a tap and the rules for the storage may prohibit cleaning your vehicle on site.

In that case, your easiest option is to find a motorhome cleaning station near you, perhaps at a local garage.

CAUTION: I wouldn't recommend using a 'drive-through' car cleaning place. Most of the people who work there have no idea about the vulnerable areas on motorhomes, campervans or caravans and will probably cause a lot of damage when they aim their pressure washer at the back of your fridge through the vent. Just trust me when I say you're better off cleaning your own van or hiring a specialist company to do it for you.

Cleaning the Roof

Most motorhomes and campervans have roofs which you can't safely walk on. Of course, some roofs have been reinforced, but most motorhomes and campers are not designed to take the weight of a normal person.

So you need another way of getting up there, like a ladder or some form of solid scaffolding. Some truck washes have a structure set up to allow you access to the roof.

Don't forget you need a ladder at or slightly taller than the height of your van. If your motorhome is 3m high, ideally get a ladder at least 3.5m high. You might not climb all the way to the top, but it will be a little more stable for you. Alternatively, some people have a permanently fitted ladder on the back of their van.

Start up at the roof, put up your ladder (you can use pipe lagging or insulation to stop it marking your motorhome and prevent slippage.) Ideally, get someone to hold the base for you.

Rinse down using a gentle scrub to loosen dirt. Warm water is nicer for you but isn't essential for cleaning if you can't get any.

Apply your motorhome cleaner to your brush, start at one end or one side and work in smooth strokes across the roof. You want to apply some pressure to lift the dirt and marks and clean around any obstacles, like solar panels.

Don't try to reach too far in case you overbalance. Keep moving the ladder as needed.

Rinse using a hose or buckets, then clean again around solar panels or obstacles, as dirty water and grime could have got stuck there after the first rinse-down.

If you have an awning, make sure you clean the top and sides of this too.

Cleaning the Sides/ Rest of Van

Repeat the process on the sides. Rinse down, then apply a general cleaner to each panel with a soft brush, microfibre cloth or mitt. Let the cleaner rest for up to 10 minutes before cleaning off with another mop, brush, or sponge.

Clean the windows. Use a sponge or mitt to initially wash, then clean off with a microfibre cloth. On the cab windows, use a glass cleaner to add shine and add Rainex. For the habitation windows, double check in the user manual what the best product is to use on the window, as most are plastic, not glass.

Dry the van, using a microfibre cloth. Get the biggest one you possibly can! You can let it dry naturally, but it risks leaving streaks.

Clean the wheels but be careful to use an appropriate cleaner to avoid damage to the brakes.

Once you've applied wheel cleaner, use a wheel brush to get rid of dirt between the spokes, then rinse.

Finally, apply polish or finishing wax for shine and to make future cleanings easier. Apply it using a flat mop or cloth. You can also add an overwintering spray to help repel dirt and algae if your polish/ wax doesn't already do this.

Can You Pressure Wash a Motorhome?

Yes, you can pressure wash a motorhome BUT with caution. We've used a pressure washer many times on our van, both at home and at a DIY garage car wash.

However, you need to be very VERY careful where you point that high-power water. Unlike a car, your motorhome has many things which do not react well to water, like the air vents for the fridge and oven. There are also seals and sealants that aren't designed to stand up to high pressure washing, especially on older vans.

If you do decide to use a pressure wash on your motorhome, be careful of:

- Being too close. The further away you stand, the less powerful the spray will be.
- Aiming at seals and sealants around windows, doors, and exterior lockers. (The older the vehicle, the less flexible and more brittle these seals are- meaning they may have cracks that

will allow water behind them- or they may break up completely.

- Spraying the water into the vents, especially at the back of the fridge or oven.
- Causing damage to motorhome TV aerials or other items on the roof.

How Often Should You Clean a Motorhome or Campervan?

That depends on how much you use it and also where it's kept. If you return from a trip and the van is particularly dirty, a good clean is better than leaving it sitting dirty.

Also, if you store or have parked your van near trees, you'll want to clean it more often, as the sap can cause damage (not to mention any bird droppings.) The same applies to salt from the sea if you're near the coast.

Caring for Your Leisure Battery

Remember all those pages ago when we spoke about your battery being like a bucket of water?

Now, as well as a bucket of water, think of your battery like a pampered dog. It wants to be warm (but not TOO warm), dry, given attention, fed often and given lots of time off to sleep.

(I have a cocker spaniel curled up on my lap right now and believe me, the analogy is working!)

The average life of a motorhome leisure battery is about 5 years, but to last that long you need to look after it regularly, especially during winter or when it's not being used often. Here are some tips to get the most out of your leisure battery.

Do:

- Charge your battery after purchase. Remember, they're discharging while just sitting there on the shelf in Halfords (or whatever store you bought it from).
- Make sure you install the battery correctly, keeping it upright and properly secured (most motorhomes have straps for this).
- Use high-quality clamps for a good connection. If you're not sure, ask the place you buy it from to fit it for you.
- Keep the terminals clean and free from corrosion. Some people add a light coat of Vaseline / petroleum jelly; we don't but we do check the terminals regularly.
- Make sure you know which appliances are constantly drawing on the battery. Trackers, alarms, security systems, rear-view cameras, Wi-Fi dongles or the clock on the dashboard are all common culprits.
- Regularly check the water levels in the battery if it's not a sealed battery. You do this by unscrewing the caps and making sure the electrolyte level covers the lead plates. If not, top up with deionised water as required. Always wear full safety equipment when inspecting and maintaining the battery– that stuff is corrosive!
- Make sure the gas relief tube remains securely in place.

- Recharge the battery once it reaches 50% power. Never allow a battery to completely run down as this can damage the battery / greatly reduce the lifespan.
- If you aren't going to be using the battery for a while, give it a properly good charge and then store it in a cool environment with an appropriate charger. You can leave in the van if you have an intelligent charging system or a trickle charger.

Don't:

- Leave your battery in a discharged state for a long period of time. If you've been using the battery, make sure it is charged up again before you leave it in storage/ unused. If you don't do this, a white deposit will form on the plates and the battery will be unusable (this is called sulphation)
- Over-charge your leisure battery. A fully charged 12V battery should have a voltage of 12.7V. Overcharging can be just as bad as undercharging for damaging a battery.
- Over-discharge your battery. If the voltage falls to 11.70V charge it immediately! If it gets much lower, you may not be able to save it.
- Reverse the polarity on your charging leads, this can damage the battery.
- Let anything fall across the battery terminals. A 12V battery is unlikely to cause electrocution, but if the terminals or the cables short-out, it can cause a fire in your motorhome.
- Forget that a lead-acid battery contains ACID. I've seen it burn through jeans when my

husband accidentally spilt some. Be careful and keep well away from kids and pets.

- Store your battery anywhere too warm, (like by a radiator, or in direct sunlight).

How do you fix a battery which won't hold a charge?

There are times when, despite your best efforts, things don't go to plan. Usually, the biggest problem is charging, either getting the battery to take a charge or getting it to hold on to the charge.

A trickle charger is the best way to try to fix a leisure battery that will not hold a charge. Slow and steady allows it to build up, but it won't be as fast as you are used to and may never regain that ability. This could be a sign it's time to change the battery.

Unless it's been run too low, in which case, see below.

How do you revive a leisure battery?

If you've accidentally run your battery too low, slow charge it for at least 24 hours and see if it revives. You can do this via a battery charger or plugging the van into the mains/ electric supply on a campsite.

Take the battery out of your camper, connect it to a decent battery charger, leave it on trickle charge for a couple of days (3-4 amps), then check the voltage. If it's not rising, the battery is probably unfixable, and you will need to replace it.

Maintaining your leisure battery during Winter

Sadly, most people only discover they have a problem with either their starter battery or their leisure battery when they return to their vehicle after a few months. Normally this is after winter (although if we ever get another lockdown, there's always a chance you might not use your motorhome as much as you planned!)

The worst time is winter, where you often have both lack of use (time while the battery quietly discharges) and cold (which makes the battery miserable.)

The two together mean that the battery discharges more quickly and is even more reluctant to recover afterwards.

Tips for maintaining your leisure battery over winter:

Give it a good charge before you put it away for winter

Leave it with some form of trickle charger. However, leaving it plugged into mains for months might damage the battery too. (The standard on-board charger in many motorhomes can also cause over-charging).

If you have an intelligent battery charging unit (which monitors the battery and adjusts charging voltage and current), you can leave that plugged in all winter.

If you are unable to attach a charger permanently (such as in storage), either charge your leisure battery once a month or remove it from the vehicle, bring it home and put it on charge. Of course, be careful if this means your alarm/ tracker becomes disabled.

Make sure it doesn't get too cold. If your battery is stored internally, the motorhome shell should stop it getting really cold. If the battery is stored in external storage, you might want to remove it from the vehicle completely until the weather warms up.

If you are storing the van at home and have a power supply, you can put it on a timer (4/5 hours a day), so it doesn't overcharge.

You can use a solar panel to provide charge to your battery. Just be aware that solar panels are less effective in winter (weaker sunlight). Also, if you use a motorhome cover it may cover the solar panel, making it useless.

Bad smell when charging

Occasionally, you might experience a 'rotten egg' smell when your battery is charging. This usually indicates that the battery is being overcharged.

The smell comes from gasses being emitted. These gasses could potentially ignite and cause explosions.

If you get this smell, check if the battery feels hot to the touch. If it does, the battery is being overcharged and could be irreparably damaged.

Even without a smell, be aware of the temperature of your battery while charging as a hot battery normally means there is a problem.

Always have a window open to allow gases to escape while the battery is charging.

DO NOT disconnect the battery from the charger while it is plugged into the mains, this could cause a spark. Disconnect the mains, then remove the charger.

Motorhome Recalls

Recalls are when the manufacturer of a vehicle realises that there is an important problem and needs to fix it. Just like with cars, they issue a 'recall notice' and expect owners to contact them so the fix can be completed.

Unlike with cars, there are a lot more 'working parts' on a motorhome or campervan, so recalls are fairly common. As an example, our Swift 685 recently had a recall for the drop-down bed and for a battery issue.

Because of the high numbers of sales and trading, there's no way for manufacturers to keep track of who the current owners are, particularly for second-hand owners, so they publish the details online and rely on you to contact them.

Some manufacturers do have a database you can update with your contact details when you buy a vehicle, so you will be notified in the future should a recall be needed, but the emphasis is on you contacting them when you buy the second-hand vehicle, not the other way around.

How to find recalls on your vehicle?

The easiest way to know if there are any recalls issued for your motorhome or campervan is to head to the DVLA website and enter your van registration number.

If you have a private reg plate fitted it will still work, just enter the reg which is on the vehicle now and the DVLA will show you any updates due on that vehicle.

If you don't know the registration number or are looking at buying a vehicle, you can enter the manufacturer details. All you need is the Make, model, and year.

Remember, you are entering the MOTORHOME make, not the chassis (So SWIFT instead of FIAT).

What to Do If There Is a Recall

If it shows there is a recall for your vehicle, your first step is to phone an approved dealership (you can search for your nearest one on Google.) The recall could either be for the engine / chassis (such as Fiat) or for the motorhome habitation (i.e.- Swift). The nature of the recall will decide who you phone.

You will be asked for the VIN number (found in the engine bay or on your V5c logbook) and for all your personal details. They will then help you get the problem fixed and tell you where to go.

Some recalls are urgent, and they ask you to bring the van in asap. Others are less urgent and can be done when convenient for you.

PART 8- WINTER USE AND LONG-TERM STORAGE

There are two types of 'winterising' when it comes to motorhomes or campervans.

The first type is to prepare a vehicle for use during the winter months, if you want to go somewhere REALLY cold, like into the Alps (or ski camping, as the Europeans call it).

The second is preparing your vehicle for winter storage and not being used very much during winter (also known as 'laying up').

Motorhoming in Winter

The first Very Important Thing to know is that most motorhomes are perfectly fine to use during winter, especially a mild winter like most of the UK or Spain. So don't assume that you HAVE to stop motorhoming once it gets cold.

Despite what you might read in some Facebook groups, most UK built motorhomes are perfectly capable of being used during a 'typical' UK winter, even if it snows.

If you happen to be in your motorhome during a particularly cold spell (several days with minus temperatures), then you might need to do some extra maintenance and take precautions but otherwise you don't need to do a thing differently, except cleaning the outside of your vehicle more frequently to stop the salt / grit from corroding anything.

There are plenty of campsites all around the UK and Europe which remain open all year, or only shut for a short maintenance period in January or February. Some of our favourite trips have been during this quiet time, although you do need to accept that the weather may be less than optimal and many seasonal attractions might be closed.

You'll also be doing your van a favour. Motorhomes are built onto the chassis of working vehicles and vehicles like these do not like being stood for long periods of time. Not being used can sometimes cause problems, so continuing to use them can be beneficial.

Of course, if you plan to take your motorhome up into mountains, whether that's Scotland or the Alps, or you want to head up to Norway in mid-winter, then you might need to do much more preparation before you leave.

There are a few things to consider if you're going to be using your van during winter:

- Tyres
- Insulation / Heating
- Vehicle checks
- Driving in bad weather.
- Condensation

If you don't think you'll use your van during the winter months, then we highly recommend 'shutting it down', which means draining the system and preparing it not to be used for a while. We go through that later in this section.

Tyres

If you plan to use your vehicle all year, it's worth putting all-season tyres onto your van. Alternatively (if you have space at home), you could get a spare set of wheels and have one set of summer tyres and one set of winter ones, which works well if you won't be doing too many miles each year.

If you think about how difficult driving your car becomes in heavy rain, ice or snow, then consider this with a much larger, heavier vehicle. it's easy to see why the right tyres with additional grip are so important.

Insulation / Heating

All manufactured motorhomes and campers have some level of insulation already built into their design. This insulation is 'graded' into different levels, so you know how well a van SHOULD do in cold temperatures.

Most modern motorhomes and campers now have Grade III Thermal Insulation and heating, which is the highest rating (given by the NCC). Grade 3 means that your systems will still work up to -15°C, and that the heating system can start up at -15°C and then raising the temperature in the habitation area up to 20°C within 4 hours. (And then the thermal efficiency is capable of keeping it there!)

HOWEVER, it's important to realise that Grade III does NOT mean 'winterised'. Many vans have a grade 3 rating and yet still have underslung tanks (which means they could freeze) and have pipes which are not insulated.

So, if you're planning on taking your vehicle somewhere REALLY cold during winter, you're possibly going to need to add additional insulation, plus some other safety gear.

You'll probably need to add additional insulation to:

- External water tanks and pipework (It's worth adding some to internal water tanks too if you can).
- Any pipework which runs along the floor (that's most of it!)
- Wheel arches
- The floor, try to create a 'double floor' effect where you can, or use carpet pieces.

Essential Gear to Take

There are some things you NEED to carry and some things you SHOULD carry if you're going somewhere where you're likely to encounter extreme cold and snow.

This is not an exhaustive list, but a good starting list includes:

- Snow chains (essential), make sure you get the right size for your tyres & know how to fit them!
- Winter / all-season tyres
- Long-handled sturdy brush (for getting snow off the roof).
- Window vac (we love our Karcher)
- A shovel (yes, for digging your vehicle out of the snow!)
- Thermal screen– ideally one with a 'turn down' to let light in.
- Anti-freeze coolant/ windscreen wash.
- Motorhome draft skirting (or a tarp).
- Insulation for pipework, external tanks, floor, windows… and anything else you can think of!)

- Bucket for collecting grey wastewater-collapsible is good as it probably needs to be shallow.

Vehicle Checks.

Make sure you check the following before you leave:

- Tyres, including condition, tread and pressure.
- Battery
- Engine Coolant / Anti-freeze
- Wiper blades, screen-wash and heated windscreen.
- Lights- make sure they're all working.

Waste & Water

When you park up, place an external bucket or container under the grey waste drain, and leave the drain open. This helps prevent freezing in the pipes. Be sure to empty the bucket regularly!

Most Aires will have places to dispose of grey and black waste (also known as chemical waste), although not all facilities are available all the time.

Many aires and campsites will leave a freshwater tap running, so that it doesn't freeze. We also suggest using a water filter for ANY campsite water.

Power & Heating

Many campsites in the mountains don't have 16-amp electricity supply, so your electric heating might not work as well as you are used to. It also means you need to be selective about how much electricity you are using at once (you don't want to be THAT van which is constantly tripping everyone's electric).

Gas heating is great, but it uses a lot of gas. We get through a 6kg bottle in about 3 days. We highly recommend fitting refillable gas bottles in your motorhome if you're going to be travelling in Europe a lot, so make sure you know where the nearest supply is (and if it stays open during winter!)

Diesel heating is also a great option, but many vans don't come with it as standard. If you do fit it, be aware of the weight, how it affects your motorhome payload and warranty.

Don't forget, you will need somewhere to dry wet gear. It helps if you have a bathroom with heating. String a line across the top and hang everything up to dry overnight.

Solar

You can't rely on solar power during winter in the same way you can at other times of the year. The sun isn't as strong, there are more hours of darkness and more areas of shade. Also, you'll be using more power than you might normally, with lights and heating on longer, plus making more hot drinks and meals.

If you already have a solar panel fitted, then by all means use what you can, but don't rely on it as your only power source.

Finding Places to Stay During Winter

It can be difficult to find places to stay in the usual way during winter if you're going up into mountains. Many roads are closed due to snow and many sites and aires close.

You also need to know what facilities they have open during winter and how many spaces will be available (Aires can change from having 140+ spaces available in summer to less than 50 in winter, due to heavy snow and not being able to clear every spot!)

One good option is to use snomadsites.com which caters for winter motorhoming and has more information than you could even think to ask!

Our motorhome in the snow at Mont Dore aire, central France.

Driving in Heavy Rain / Bad Weather

According to Highways England, people are 30 times more likely to be killed or injured on the roads when it is raining, rather than in snow or icy conditions.

Even doing the speed limit can be dangerous in rain, especially very heavy rain. The most important thing is how much space you leave between you and the vehicle in front. Stopping distances are increased substantially (over twice as long) when the road surface is wet- that's assuming you can stop and the vehicle doesn't just aquaplane if you brake too hard.

There is no hard or fast rule saying how much slower you should drive in the rain. Some countries, like France, have two speed limits on their major motorways; one for normal weather and one for rainy conditions (130km vs 110km / hour).

Some tips for driving in bad weather:

- Replace the blades on your windshield wipers.
- Upgrade your windshield wiper fluid to one which naturally aids your windshield in repelling water (or add Rainex).
- Check tyres for adequate tread / fit winter tyres.
- Check tyre pressure is correct.
- Ensure all vehicle lights are working: headlights, brake lights, indicators, fog lights and hazard lights.

TOP TIP: Don't rely on a clever vehicle system to tell you when a bulb is out, check them manually before your next trip.

There are also several safety precautions which should be observed when driving in bad weather, including:

Use your headlights and your wipers. Not only will using these help you to see better but having your headlights on will make you more visible to other drivers.

Drive more slowly than usual. No matter what the speed limit sign says, slow down until you are comfortable. This will also keep you from hydroplaning on standing water you may come across. But don't hog the middle lane!

Leave lots of braking room between you and the vehicle in front of you. During rain, it is recommended to leave at least 2 vehicle lengths.

Do not brake hard. This is another way to skid across the road, or hydroplane. You can lose control of your vehicle in this situation and end up in an accident. Apply pressure gently and build up slowly.

Try and avoid standing water; this is the easiest way to avoid aquaplaning. If you can, follow the 'tracks' of the vehicle ahead of you. (For reference- hydroplaning & aquaplaning are the same thing- skidding across the top of water in a terrifying and not-very-controllable way!)

If you do hydroplane, react calmly. Do not slam on your brakes or yank the wheel. Instead, come off the accelerator and try to carefully yet firmly keep your car headed in the direction it is supposed to go.

Use built-in ventilation options to de-fog your windows. If you cannot see, pull over to avoid an accident.

Do not use cruise control. If you accidentally hydroplane, cruise control will make the vehicle go faster. It is best to be in control of as much of the vehicle as you can during rainy weather.

Take extra precautions when merging. Your visibility will be more limited, so make use of all your mirrors and be sure to check over your shoulder. If someone is in the van with you, they can help look for cars. Clearly signal before you move over.

Check and check AGAIN for motorcyclists. They are easily hidden by rain spray. Make sure you indicate clearly and wait a couple of seconds before you change lanes.

Give large trucks or buses extra space. If you follow them too closely, you will get caught in the wake of their tyres. All the water splashing up off the road will greatly decrease your visibility.

Be aware that roads will have a glare at night and may affect your visibility. Slow down when approaching oncoming vehicles, as the glare from their lights will also decrease your visibility.

If there's a storm with lightning, keep in mind that you will feel temporarily blinded by these lights and adjust your speed accordingly.

Always be looking ahead of where you are so you have time to anticipate potential problems.

Minimising Condensation / Mildew / Mould

Condensation, mould and mildew are constant sources of frustration to many motorhome and campervan owners. Over the years, especially when living on boats, we've tried all sorts to reduce or stop them.

Condensation is a problem because the moisture on the windows can drip down and cause damp patches on the walls. It can also drip from places like the windscreen into areas with sensitive electronics, which don't enjoy getting wet!

Mould and mildew have spores which release into the atmosphere and affect the air you are breathing. This can cause damage to your lungs and overall health. It also causes that 'musty' smell, which is just plain unpleasant. The bad news is that the spores are often invisible to the naked eye…!

Mould is microscopic fungi which lives off any organic matter. It loves warm, humid environments. Mildew is a type of mould and grows in spaces where there is a high level of moisture, like a shower.

Moisture in a motorhome can be caused by many things: cooking, showers, humidity, spills, leaks, damage and even breathing! The good news is that if you eliminate as much moisture as possible, you can eliminate much of the danger of mould and mildew.

Here are some tips to eliminate moisture in your van, especially during the winter months when things stay damp a lot longer:

Keep it warm

This is our preferred solution to stop condensation on both the boat and in our motorhome and it works, although it will increase your electric / gas use.

Keeping your space at a comfortable temperature stops the air cooling down enough to cause condensation. I should point out that when it gets REALLY cold outside, this no longer works so well.

Open a window

A simple solution is to open a window. (This is not always a fun solution- especially if it's cold and/ or raining!) However, allowing in fresh air with less water vapour reduces the humidity levels and therefore reduces the level of condensation which can occur. There's no set rule on how long you should have the window open for but obviously the longer the better.

We always open a window or a vent whenever we are cooking so the humid air from cooking can dissipate. Heating from cooking generally involves steam, which contains- you guessed it- moisture!

Create Airflow

Similarly, you need to get airflow into lockers, cupboards and wardrobes in order to avoid damp, mould and mildew. We try to keep leave things open when we're not using the van. Don't forget, mildew also affects paperwork and books, so be careful what you leave onboard when you're not using your van.

You also need airflow around your cushions and seats, so make sure to pull them out a little so that you don't come back to seats covered in horrible green spots. You can also cut small holes or fit a vent to allow airflow to cupboards which don't already have them.

Use an extractor fan/ vent

For the same reasons as above, if you have an extractor fitted either in your bathroom or kitchen, use it to freshen up the air, especially after a shower or while cooking.

Showers are the hardest. So much hot, moist air which needs to go somewhere. We don't have an extractor fan, so we leave our bathroom roof vents open for a couple of hours after a shower and keep the bathroom door shut as much as possible so that air doesn't get out into the rest of the motorhome.

Use Campsite facilities if available

As mentioned many times already, we LOVE to wild parkup with our motorhome. BUT, in winter, we use campsites a lot more, so that we're not steaming up our van with hot showers.

Keep things dry

In winter, we try hard to avoid anything damp coming into the van. However, that's often difficult with two adults who enjoy walks…and a spaniel. We hang any wet clothes or boots in our bathroom, which has a heater outlet. And we have a doggy bag for the dog, which helps enormously with drying him off.

Put a protector over your windows

This works exactly like double-glazing; you have a buffer between the cold surface and the warm air inside the motorhome. There are several way to achieve it. We've found the easiest is a thermal screen on the outside of the cab, this works brilliantly. I've heard of some people fitting an extra layer inside their windows too, but we've not tried this.

NOTE- the pull-over fitted screens inside the cab are great for privacy, but don't stop condensation as the air just circulates around them.

Check for leaks

It's probably common sense, but if your van is leaking, you're going to get more moisture into your space. Moisture = condensation when it's warmed up, so make sure there are no leaks. We carry a tube of silicone and some seals with us- just in case.

Use a dehumidifier

We don't use plug-in dehumidifiers on the motorhome, but we do on the boat, and they work great. If you have the storage space, payload, and electric capabilities, you can use a dehumidifier whilst you're using the van.

Also, you could leave one plugged in for a while whilst the van is not in use if it's on your drive or somewhere with electric. Just remember that dehumidifiers need emptying regularly and don't leave it plugged in / turned on full time.

Laying Up for Winter

There are two main reasons we recommend shutting down your motorhome for winter if you're not using it for a while and / or putting it into storage.

The first reason is to avoid problems from the cold, like damp, mould and burst pipes. Most damage done to motorhomes occurs during the cold winter months. Cold weather can also cause problems with tyres, seals, engines and other essential parts.

The second reason is to comply with many motorhome insurance policies, which usually state that they will not cover damage caused by water freezing inside the motorhome systems (including heating) between November and March. (Check your insurance policy to know exactly what rules you need to comply with).

If you won't be using your van during winter, I recommend following the steps below as soon as it starts to get frosty so you avoid potential problems, particularly if the weather is going to be approaching 0°c and things might start to freeze!

Where to store a motorhome for winter

If you don't have a permanent motorhome storage place and can't keep the van at home, you'll need to find and book a storage spot as soon as possible- they get booked up quickly.

Many farmers offer barns for indoor, covered storage and there are plenty of secure outdoor motorhome storage places around- just Google for your area.

Personally, I would try to find somewhere not too far away, so you can visit it regularly.

If you are storing your camper at home, make sure to fit some additional motorhome security devices– thefts of motorhomes (and other vehicles) increase over winter, especially in the run-up to Christmas.

If you want to keep your motorhome battery on charge, you may have to take it home with you- many motorhome storage units don't have or allow electricity to be connected to your van.

They also often don't allow you to wash or drain down your system on site, so you'll have to do that elsewhere (like a campsite).

How to store a motorhome for the winter

This section may all sound overwhelming, but I promise it's not that bad. A little effort now will save a lot of trouble in a few months' time.

Step 1- Empty nearly everything out

Empty out all perishables (food, drinks etc). We often leave our canned foods in the motorhome, but we do remove any fizzy drinks, just in case! Remember to remove spices, flour etc as these can attract bugs if left.

Remove ALL linens and clothes. Anything which can easily mould. This includes coats, towels, bedding, mattress & seat cushions. Some people remove their curtains too- we never have but it's personal preference.

We also remove toilet and kitchen rolls, which only go soggy if left behind.

All personal hygiene soaps, liquids, and sanitary protection.

Take out ALL valuables, especially electronics. Remove sat-navs, speakers, torches, battery lights, fairy lights- we often find the battery terminals can corrode if left too long in the cold/ damp.

Remove motorhome books, magazines, photos and any other paper-based product. If you have a motorhome logbook or journal, remove that too. (If you don't have one, we highly recommend one! Grab one of ours on the Wandering Bird website.

You can leave the owner's manual in over winter if you wish, but there's a chance it could get damaged.

Step 2- What can I leave in my motorhome over the winter?

It's ok to leave some things inside your van over winter. Admittedly, some things will depend upon whether you're leaving it plugged in and leaving any heating on, but here's a helpful guide for you of things we leave in the van over winter.

(By heating, I mean something like an oil filled radiator if you have electricity. Don't leave your van heating on all winter- it will break.)

- Pots/ pans (cleaned!)
- Crockery/ cutlery/ glassware (cleaned!)
- Motorhome cleaning supplies (you can choose to remove the liquids if you wish. We never have, but then we don't live anywhere it gets REALLY cold)

- Some people choose to leave their first aid kit/ medicines. We remove ours, but that's only so we can use it over winter and things don't go out of date.
- Games- although we remove cards
- Motorhome generator (drained)
- Dog bowls/ toys (because you know you'll forget them otherwise!)
- Smoke alarm/ carbon monoxide detector (yes, with batteries in. Just in case
- You can leave your TV or other electronics but remember thieves could target them.

Step 3- Cleaning

Once everything is out, give it all a REALLY good clean, inside and out.

- Check your awning is totally dry before storing it away.
- Check the fridge/ freezer are empty & clean. Leave the door hooked ajar (there's often a locking setting on the fridge door catch which you can pull out to do this).
- Prevent against condensation & mould. Leave all lockers, cupboards, wardrobes etc ajar.
- Top things up.

This is a good time to apply a coat or two of wax to the outside.

Once you've emptied and cleaned, think about the things you are leaving behind and top up any fluids which will be staying in the vehicle, including:

- LPG Gas cylinders. It might be best to remove them completely and store them at home (yes, you're going to lose your spare bedroom for the winter!) This is also a good time to TURN OFF all gas bottles and also the main supply into the motorhome.
- Put antifreeze in the engine (we'll get to using antifreeze inside your motorhome plumbing in a bit).
- Engine Oil
- Motorhome Fuel
- Check tyre pressure (also check tread and make sure there is no cracking/ damage before winter starts- cold weather won't help that at all!)

How to drain down your camper

DISCLAIMER: This is a generic guide. Most motorhome systems are very similar, but please do check your owner's manual before following these steps. If in doubt, ask your dealership or a local garage for advice on your specific model.

Empty ALL systems over a suitable drainage point. (If you can, angle your motorhome on chocks to get as much water as possible out).

Make sure you have emptied all: freshwater, wastewater, water heater tank and toilet flush (if separate from freshwater).

You can use a water heater bypass kit instead if you wish. There are also kits which 'blow' through the system to get all residual water out.

- Make sure your toilet is empty.
- Open all internal taps (yep, while over the drain)- LEAVE these open all winter.
- If you have a mixer tap, leave it open in the middle so both sides are on.
- If you have inline water filters, disconnect and empty these.
- Leave the water pump running until taps run dry (then turn it off quickly to avoid pump burnout).
- Remove the showerhead and drain water from the hose. Leave the hose hanging onto the bathroom drain (if you have a wet-room / shower room) or a bowl if you have carpet.
- Check underneath the motorhome and make sure the u-bends are as empty as possible (this is normally where the shower u-bends are).
- If possible, go for a quick drive to bump things around and make sure everything is as clear of water as possible.

Also, don't forget diesel and petrol have a shelf life. Now is the time to check your motorhome generator, motorbikes, spare fuel tanks or anything else in the van which uses fuel and either drain it down completely or check the fuel to be sure it's still ok.

Should you use antifreeze?

If you don't use a drainage kit, there may be some water left in your 'u' bends. You can add a little antifreeze down the plughole to help stop this water freezing (especially in sinks).

DON'T add antifreeze to your freshwater pipe unless it's a special motorhome antifreeze which is non-toxic!

Should you cover your motorhome in winter?

Ideally, you want to store your motorhome or campervan indoors during winter. If that's not possible then yes, a motorhome cover is a good idea. The more layers of insulation the motorhome has, the better.

However, be sure that you use a breathable cover, otherwise the air won't circulate, and you'll cause mould and mildew. (Be warned, winter covers are NOT easy to put on!!) You also want to make sure you get one which fits your vehicle and allows access to the habitation door.

Some people just choose to cover their windscreen and you might choose to leave your wiper blades hinged away from the windscreen so they can't freeze in place.

Other tips

If you can connect to power, leave a small heater on low / night-time setting to guard against freezing.

Fit exterior vents to fridges and leave fridge door open.

Leave cabinets and interior doors open to allow air to circulate.

You can spray a little WD-40 on catches, locks and some electrics to prevent rust or corrosion.

Ensure all protective systems are working ok- alarms, trackers etc.

Protect your motorhome from rodents - The biscuit test!

It's a sad fact that a van left alone for a while will attract various animals looking for a home. Mice, rats and spiders can all move in during your absence, and then can hide in one of a million places.

One of the best tricks to see if anything has moved in is the biscuit test.

Put a tiny piece of biscuit on the floor in the motorhome when you leave it for winter. If it's still there when you return, you don't have any mice or rats as residents!

Sadly, we don't have any good tricks to deter spiders. Conkers, laundry sheets and blocking holes with tissue may help but don't forget you need to leave some ventilation into the van… which means holes. Vicious circle, unfortunately.

Jobs to do DURING Winter

Once your motorhome is prepared and tucked up for the winter, you can't just forget about it for 5 months. In order to prevent issues after being stood for long periods, you need to do the following at least once a month if possible:

- Check on your motorhome if it's not parked near you.
- Look for signs of mould, mildew or damp and deal with any potential problems ASAP. Leaving it will only make it worse!
- Start the engine and ideally go for a short drive (at least 20 minutes).

- Leave the gearbox in neutral if possible and / or don't apply the handbrake while parked. Alternatively, alternate between the two to try and limit wear. (This is when wheel wedges are useful).
- If you can't drive the vehicle, run the engine for 30 minutes and rev in one-minute intervals once it's warm (this is not as good as driving it, and may cause build-up).
- Turn the air-conditioning on (ideally, while you're driving.) I know it's winter and cold, but this really helps keep the system ticking over for whenever you next need it.
- Move the vehicle slightly so it's not constantly on the same patch of tyre. Alternatively, use tyre savers to take the weight off, especially if your motorhome is over 3.5 tonnes.
- Tyre covers can be useful to protect the brake discs.

Things to do AFTER Winter

Finally, FINALLY, winter comes to an end and it's time to start preparing for your next motorhome holiday. But, before you set off, there are some important things to check and do:

- Reconnect anything which was disconnected, like the battery.
- Check the battery is still serviceable. If in doubt, get it checked professionally.
- Close any pipes left open.

- Remove any vent covers, skirting or motorhome covers.
- Check tyre pressure and drive vehicle to make sure there are no 'flat spots'.
- Do a full engine check, including oil and water levels.
- Give your engine a good run.
- Fill fuel and gas.
- Get a habitation check done or check all systems are working.
- Get your motorhome clean inside and out and be ready for the new season.

Preparing your van for winter/ extended storage

PART 9- SELLING YOUR MOTORHOME

At some point, you'll probably consider selling your motorhome. Either you'll realise it was completely the wrong layout for you (which is what happened with our first motorhome), or you'll decide to upsize or downsize (which is what we did after our second!)

Or you might decide that motorhoming is no longer for you and move on to other hobbies.

Ways to Sell Your Motorhome

Broadly speaking, there are 4 main ways to sell your motorhome or camper:

To a dealer - either in part exchange or sometimes outright. You may have more luck with getting them to take it outright during the summer when there is more demand, and a dealer has more chance of selling your old motorhome on.

Via a broker - A broker will try to sell your van for you on a 'sale or return' basis. If they sell the vehicle, they will take a commission, but they will also deal with the task of advertising, meeting potential buyers, test drives, paperwork and all the other difficult parts about selling a vehicle.

Privately - Selling privately (via online or an advert) is still a popular choice and you have two main ways to do this - Online or physical advertising. Or word of mouth I suppose.

There are plenty of websites, forums and groups which allow you to list your motorhome for sale online. You could also put an advert in a local shop or specialist magazine. Nearly all charge a fee - some charge more than others, but these are generally more popular and reputable locations.

You will need to include lots of photos of your vehicle, and as much detail as possible. The upsides of selling privately are you can get more money. The downsides are dealing with potential buyers and potential fraudsters.

At an auction - You can list your motorhome or camper to be sold at auction. Remember that, although it will sell quickly and will usually be 'sold as seen' you are unlikely to get the best price and you must also pay a commission.

How to sell via a dealership

The first step is to contact several dealerships and ask them if they are interested in buying your vehicle. Often, they will only be interested as a part-exchange, but there are times when they'll buy it outright- if it's a sought-after model (or after a global pandemic when dealers were struggling to keep up with demand!)

The Pros of selling to a dealer is that the transaction is generally quick and easy (you don't need to deal with 'tyre-kickers' or handle 5000 phone calls), you often don't need to arrange your own habitation check and they can help you organise all the paperwork. You will probably feel more at ease dealing with a reputable dealer than a potential fraudster.

The downside is that you will rarely get as much money as you will if you sell it privately.

If you're planning to buy another van, I would always recommend using a dealer- it's so much easier and you can often get extras thrown in, like a solar panel, bike rack or awning fitted. You can also play dealers off against each other if you can find two or three with a motorhome you want to exchange for.

Expect the dealer to ask a LOT of questions when you initially contact them about a sale, things like the VIN number, mileage, condition, extras, manuals. Basically, everything a potential customer might want to know. They will probably also want to see plenty of pictures before offering you a quote.

HOWEVER, if you have bought an ex-hire vehicle, you'll find dealerships are often reluctant to take them. We made this mistake with our second van and were unable to part-ex it.

Apparently, buyers are concerned about vehicles which have been ex-hire in the past (which is silly in my opinion as we left that vehicle in a better state than we bought it in!)

So we had to sell our second vehicle privately, which wasn't the end of the world but was a snag we weren't anticipating.

It meant we had to buy the motorhome we wanted before it sold and then we ended up with two vans for a while, which was a pain for storage and insurance!

How to sell using a broker

A motorhome broker puts your motorhome onto their books and tries to find a suitable buyer. You don't get any money until they sell the motorhome and then they take their commission out of the sale price.

The advantages of selling with a broker is that you will usually get a better price than if you part-exchange with a dealer, BUT still not as much as if you sell privately (after all, they're doing all the work).

The downsides are:

- You have to wait for the vehicle to sell before you get any money.
- You might have to keep paying loans or tax (depending on terms of the broker) until it sells.
- You might have to pay for any maintenance which is needed whilst it's in the broker's care.

There are also plenty of horror stories about thieves posing as brokers and then stealing the vehicle.

Make sure you get the broker to assume all responsibility (in writing) for insurance, both for storing the vehicle and for any test drives they may do. If they can't insure it whilst in their possession, go elsewhere.

It's important to do plenty of checks before you select a broker and only go with someone who has been recommended to you or who has a set address where you can view the motorhomes on sale. Get everything in writing, including how quickly you will receive your money after the sale, what price you want to sell for (after commission), how much commission you are paying the broker etc.

We've never used a broker ourselves, but personally we'd probably choose to sell privately instead of using one.

How to sell privately

You sell a motorhome privately in much the same way as you sell a car, advertise on a site with vehicles for sale, get lots of phone calls or messages. Arrange viewings for people who are interested and then hopefully sell it quickly without any drama.

The advantages to selling privately are that you get the maximum amount of money, and you keep the vehicle, meaning you can use it whilst you're trying to sell it.

The downsides are that you have to deal with prospective buyers, phone calls, issues and timewasters.

There are many places to list a motorhome privately for sale:

- Online adverts (like Autotrader, eBay or Gumtree).
- Facebook groups which allow sales posts.
- Online Forums
- Specific motorhome website 'For Sale' sections.
- Magazine adverts, like Practical Motorhome or MMM.
- Local shops or business advertising boards.

Online advertising is probably your best bet. Most people now research and look for sales online, particularly if they don't want to use a dealership in the hope of saving money.

And that's the thing to remember - anyone who ISN'T choosing to use the safety of a dealer (who can provide things like warranties and extras), is either looking for something very specific or, most likely, they're trying to save money by avoiding inflated dealer prices.

NOTE: We do NOT recommend using eBay or Gumtree. Sure, there are some genuine sellers and buyers on there, but there are so many fraudsters it's become a complete minefield. Of course, it's your decision what you want to do, but that's our opinion.

Things to be mindful off when selling privately:

Sadly, not everyone is 'above board' and motorhomes are worth a LOT of money. There are plenty of unscrupulous people looking to take advantage of trusting sellers.

Here are some tips to combat this:

- Don't hand over any keys. Unlock doors, lockers and start the engine for them.
- Don't allow them to test-drive- drive it with them in it. You're under no obligation to give a test drive (see below).
- Don't leave anyone in the hab area unattended.
- Alarm bells should start ringing if anyone wants to buy without seeing it first, wants to have a courier collect or have you to drive it to their house. Make sure you get full, cleared payment

BEFORE you take it anywhere and be aware that some banks allow transactions to be reversed for a certain period of time. Check how long that is with your bank and ask them for advice to safeguard yourself.

Other tips for selling

- Make sure you have the electric plugged in so the buyer can see everything working.
- Show any problems and get the sale in writing with 'sold as seen' or 'subject to...' on the receipt.
- If it's winter, put the heating on, so it feels warm and cosy.
- Make sure the van is clean and clear from as many personal belongings as possible.
- Remove any extras not being sold with the van, so there's no confusion.
- Have the paperwork to hand for the buyer to look through.
- Clean it inside and out and touch up / fix as many small things as possible- the less it looks like there is to do, the less haggle room the buyer has.

Letting buyers test drive

You know how nervous you would be to purchase an expensive vehicle without test driving it first. HOWEVER, many dealers don't offer test drives because insurance is a pain.

If you do choose to allow a prospective customer to test drive your motorhome, then you MUST check their insurance and driving license covers them to drive your vehicle and you must check the terms on your insurance as well.

You should also be aware that:

- The potential buyer can only drive your motorhome on your policy if you have it set for any driver to drive OR if you add the buyer as a named driver.
- Their insurance will likely only cover them for third party risk; what if they scratch it or reverse into a wall?
- Are they legally allowed to drive a vehicle over 3.5 tonne? Ask for proof and take a photo of their driving licence.

How to get payment for your motorhome

Despite what I said earlier, the safest payment method is using direct bank transfer. Do not let it go until the money is CLEAR in your account, not just pending. Do not accept cheques or other money services.

You CAN accept PayPal IF you sold through an auction site such as eBay, but be aware that if you ended the auction early, PayPal rarely offers protection for you as the seller. Also, PayPal charges fees, which can be a lot of money on something as expensive as a motorhome.

Cash purchases sound great but be sure to use a forgery detecting pen (available from Amazon or eBay) and check EVERY. SINGLE. NOTE.

Selling at Auction

Auctions are a great way to sell and buy second-hand motorhomes and campervans. They're often used by traders for one reason; vehicles sell for well under market value. With this in mind, you're unlikely to get top price for your van, although you can specify a minimum amount, so it doesn't sell for less than that.

Remember that the auction house will take a commission, which will be a set percentage of the sale price, the more it sells for, the more you pay them. Also, selling your van is not guaranteed, especially if you have a high 'minimum' sale limit; if it's not a great deal, traders are unlikely to bite, because they can't make as much money.

There are some auctions available just for motorhomes, campers and caravans, but you can also add yours to most 'vehicle' auctions to see what happens. Google your nearest vehicle auction house and ask them for advice.

How to value your vehicle

Motorhomes are tough to value as, unlike cars, there is no definitive guide. There are so many types, models, and extras available on the market, combined with a relatively small number of the same model produced each year, with huge differences in mileage- all of which make valuing a motorhome very difficult.

Even dealers struggle: they rely mainly on past experience and what's popular with buyers right then.

Many people will tell you that your motorhome is going to be worth less than you paid for it and, to a point, they're right. Motorhomes do depreciate. However, it doesn't have to be a LOT less.

If you've taken care of your vehicle, kept up with maintenance and it still looks good (and you haven't added thousands of miles to it,) you could potentially sell it for only a little less than what you paid.

To get a starting point for valuation, call around some dealers and brokers. Even if you want to sell privately, getting a quote from them will give you a baseline (and a bottom line; if they're willing to buy your vehicle for £20,000, you don't need to sell it to anyone for less than that).

You can also check out other adverts of a similar van (as a comparison) if it's a popular model. Some sites even show past sales or auctions so you can get an idea.

Have a look at vans on dealer's forecourts: are they selling a motorhome like yours? How does it compare in terms of age, condition, layout, mileage, and extras?

NOTE: At the time of writing this, the market is insane post-Covid, and the price of vans is much much higher than normal. At some point, it will come back down again, so you might find you lose out if you bought a van during the peak. But generally, a well-maintained van should hold its value very well.

How to prepare your vehicle for sale

Whether you're selling to a dealer or privately, it's worth doing some preparation work to get your van looking as good as possible.

- Wash and wax your vehicle, including the roof and cleaning the windows. Add alloy protector to make your alloys really shine.
- Make sure water and waste outlets work- empty all tanks.
- Clean and empty toilet.
- Ensure you have all keys and that all locks work freely.
- Clear out all lockers and garage from everything you don't want to sell with the van.
- Fix any small issues, like broken light bulbs or hinges.
- Clean scuff marks as much as possible.
- Empty and clean fridge.
- Check carpets, seats and curtains.
- Hoover throughout.
- Use air freshener to stop any smells, including pet smells, food and mould.
- Test gas, electric and appliances like the fridge and cooker.
- Remove any extras you want to keep.
- Get all paperwork and manuals together- the more, the better.
- Gather all tools, specific spanners or other useful accessories in one place.
- Get a hab check unless the dealer is happy to do one.

Organising the Paperwork

Before you can sell your vehicle, you need to make sure the paperwork is in order and ready for the new buyer.

- For the best price, get a new MOT and hab check.
- If you have a private reg and want to keep it, remove it from the van in plenty of time so you can get the new paperwork through.
- Make sure the service history book has been stamped/ updated.
- Have the V5C logbook accessible.
- Keep all receipts/ manuals organised and easy to access.

After the Sale

Once you have agreed to the sale, make sure that you don't hand over the keys until the money has cleared into your account.

When you sell the motorhome, you need to fill out the New Keeper section of the V5C and send it to the DVLA to tell them you are no longer the registered keeper of the vehicle (do not rely on the new buyer to do this).

You should also organise a sales invoice, including any terms and conditions you've agreed with the buyer. Get them to sign it as proof they're happy.

Make sure you cancel your tax for the vehicle if you pay monthly. If you've paid in advance, request a rebate from the DVLA. It is the new buyer's responsibility to organise tax and insurance as soon as they become the new owner (i.e.- before they drive the vehicle home.)

CONGRATULATIONS

Phew!

If your brain isn't exploding after all that, you're doing well. I've just thrown a crazy amount of information at you and now there will be a quiz... (only joking. No quiz. Promise.)

I want you to remember what I said all the way back at the beginning of this book; it's ok not to know all this stuff straight away. What I've shared has been 4+ YEARS of nearly non-stop experience (which is probably the equivalent of about 20 years 'normal' motorhoming).

There's no way you can read this book through once and know it all and nothing compares to getting out there and doing it for yourself. So, whenever you can, just get away- even if it's just a weekend for one night. Worst case, have a night on the drive so you can test everything out.

Don't forget, if you need to buy any kit, want to see what we use or want to grab any of the checklists in a printable format, just head to:

https://www.wandering-bird.com/mms

Of course, you'll be nervous the first couple of times you do something new, but the more you learn and do, the easier it gets- and the more fun you'll have!

Next Steps

I know there's already a crazy amount of information in here. However, as you get more confident, you might be interested in trying different things.

If you'd like more guidance, including:

SCAN ME

- Travelling to Europe
- Wild parking with a van/ motorhome
- In-depth guides on France, Scotland or Wales travel

you can find them all here >>>

or at https://www.wandering-bird.com/mms

(use code **THANKS10** to get 10% off everything)

Please do let me know where you go- I'd love to see where you end up!

Feel free to join the Wandering Bird Facebook group and you can also find me on Instagram and Tiktok (@wanderingbird.adventures) where I'm always happy to answer questions.

Safe travels!

Kat x

About the Author

Kathryn Bird is an ex-air traffic controller who decided to get out of the rat race whilst she was still young enough to enjoy it.

She quit her job and now explores Europe by motorhome and motorbike, sharing her experiences on the award-winning travel blog **Wandering Bird**.

She is passionate about inspiring others to have their own adventures and experience the freedom of life on the road, whether it's a long weekend or a month away.

You can read more about Kathryn's adventures, tips and 'How to' guides at **www.wandering-bird.com** where you can also find checklists, itinerary ideas and guides to help you have your own epic adventures in your van.

Printed in Great Britain
by Amazon